FOR ORGANS, PIANOS & ELECTRONIC KEYBOARDS

E-Z PLAY TODAY

161

HENRY MANCINI

Cover Photo: CharlesBush.com

ISBN 978-1-61774-060-2

HAL•LEONARD®
CORPORATION

7777 W. BLUEMOUND RD. P.O. BOX 13819 MILWAUKEE, WI 53213

E-Z Play® Today Music Notation © 1975 by HAL LEONARD CORPORATION
E-Z PLAY and EASY ELECTRONIC KEYBOARD MUSIC are registered trademarks of HAL LEONARD CORPORATION.

Visit Hal Leonard Online at
www.halleonard.com

Anywhere the Heart Goes

from THE THORN BIRDS

Registration 8
Rhythm: Waltz

Music by Henry Mancini
Lyrics by Will Jennings

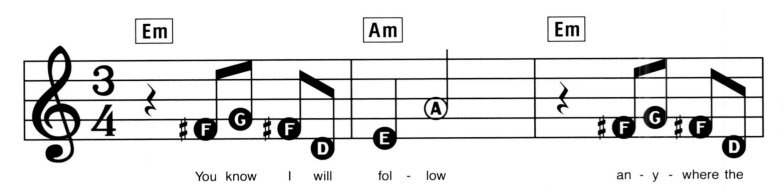

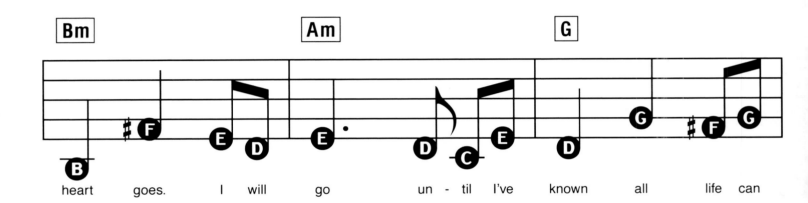

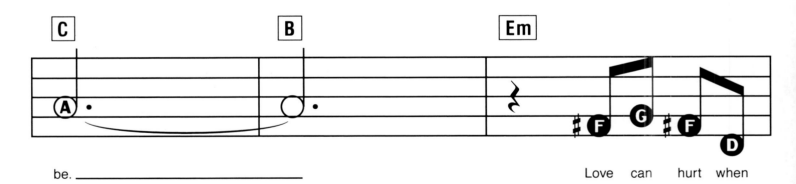

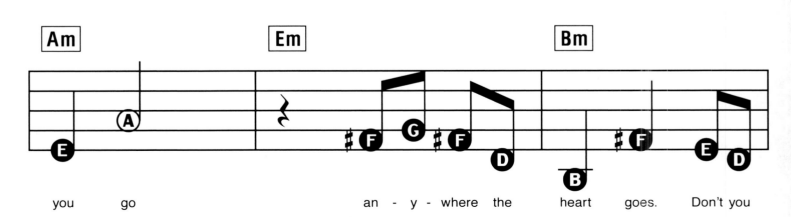

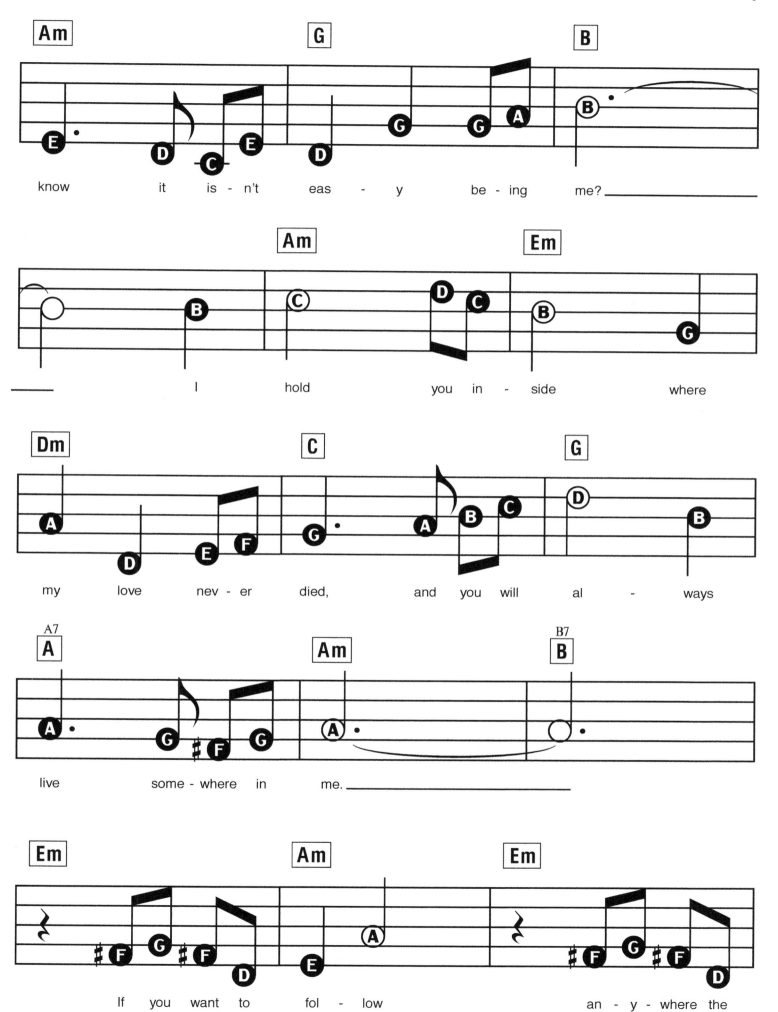

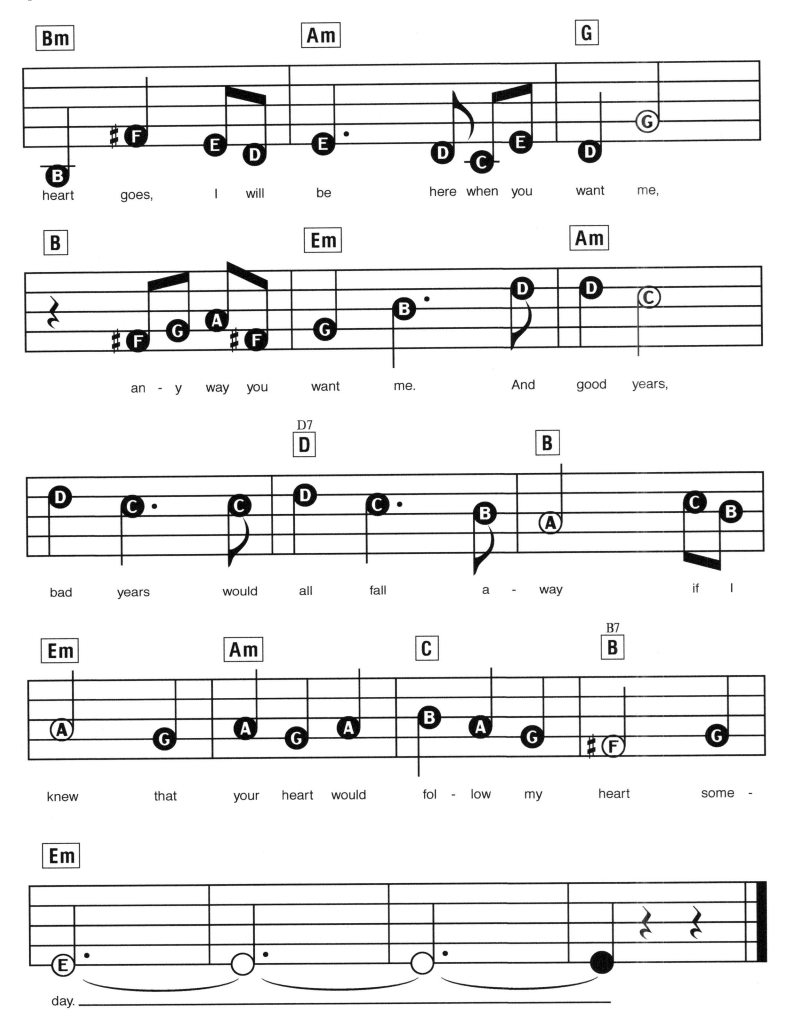

Baby Elephant Walk
from the Paramount Picture HATARI!

Registration 7
Rhythm: 8-Beat or Rock

By Henry Mancini

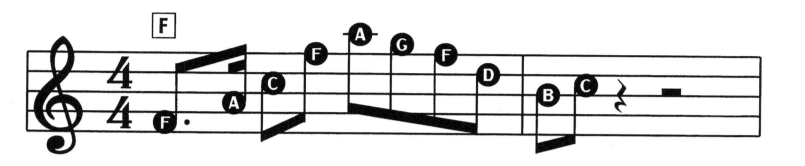

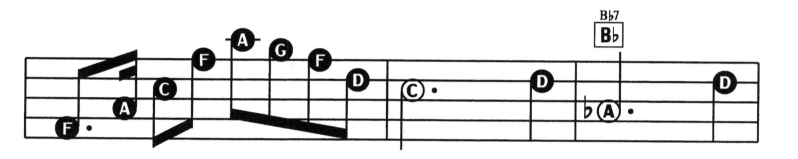

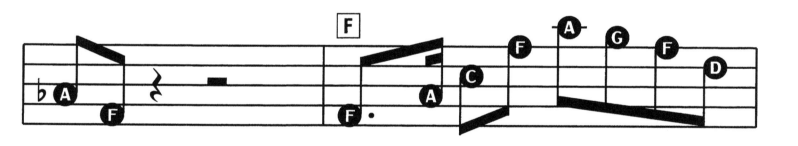

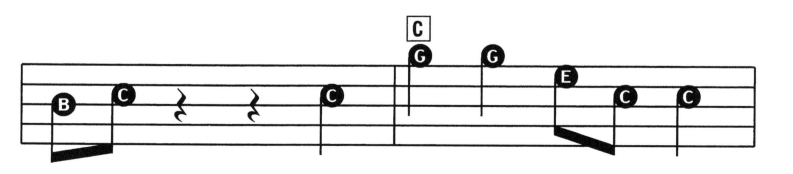

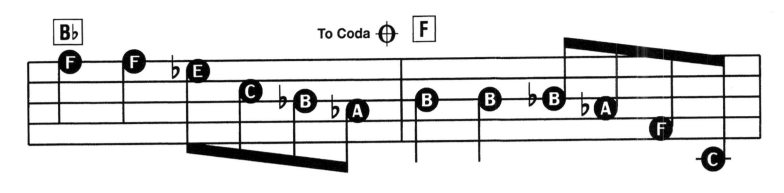

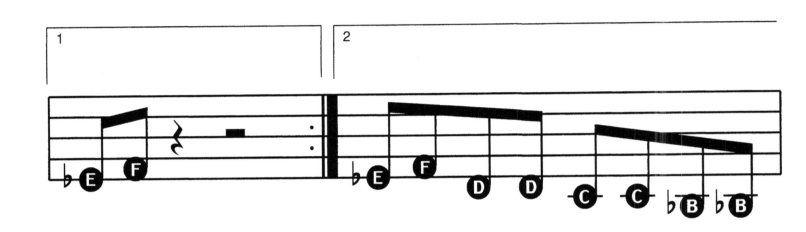

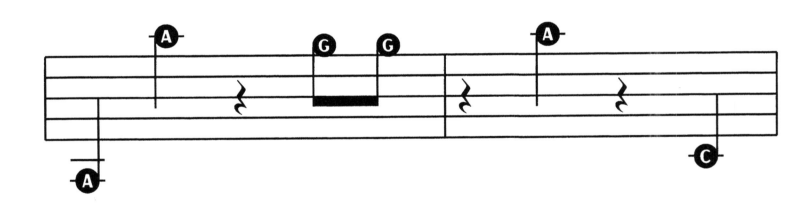

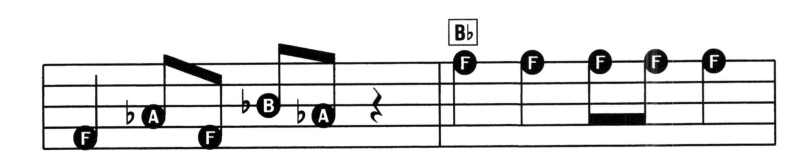

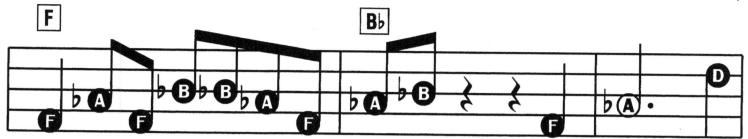

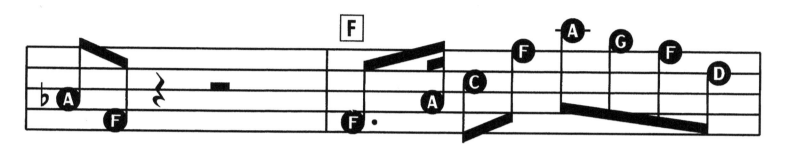

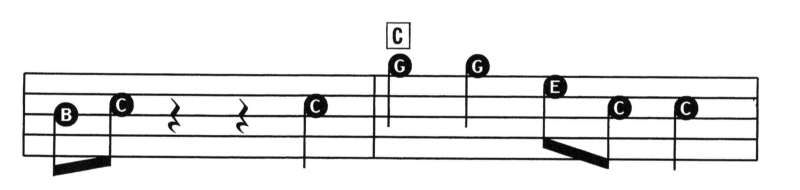

D.C. al Coda
(Return to beginning
Play to ⊕ and
Skip to Coda)

CODA

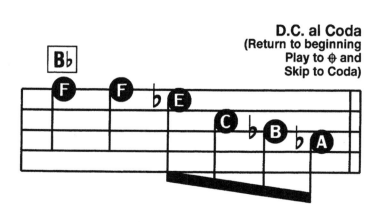

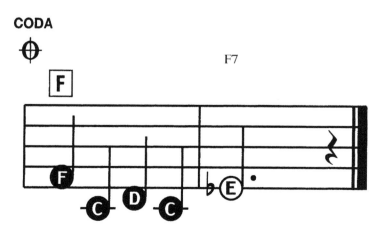

Charade
from CHARADE

Registration 3
Rhythm: Waltz

Music by Henry Mancini
Words by Johnny Mercer

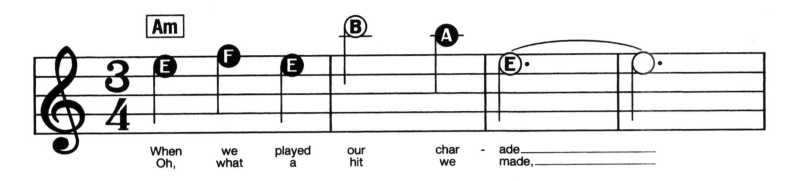

When we played our char - ade_____
Oh, what a hit we made,_____

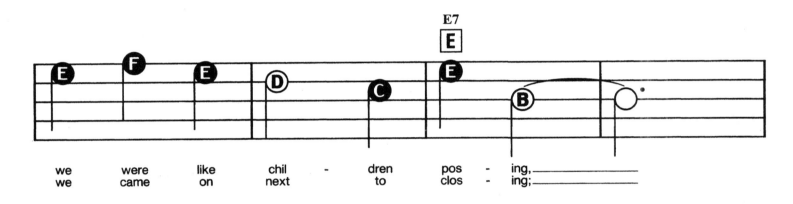

we were like chil - dren pos - ing,_____
we came on next to clos - ing;_____

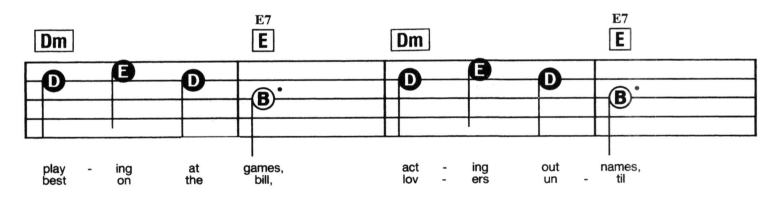

play - ing at games, act - ing out names,
best on at the bill, lov - ers un - til

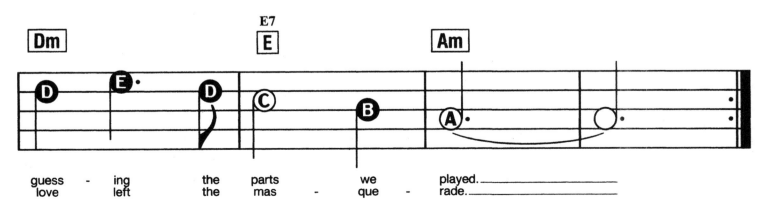

guess - ing the parts we played._____
love left the mas - que - rade._____

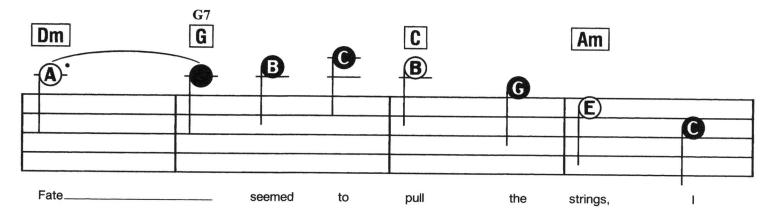

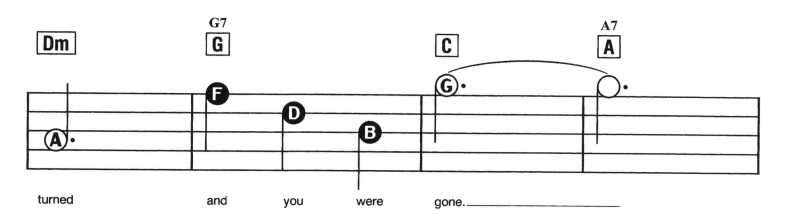

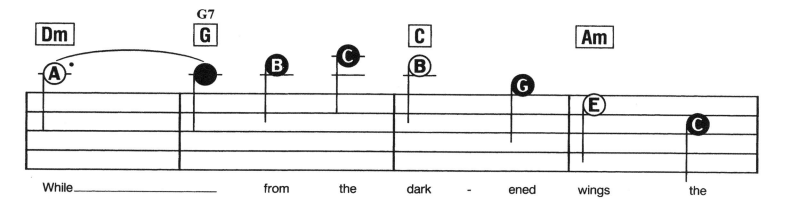

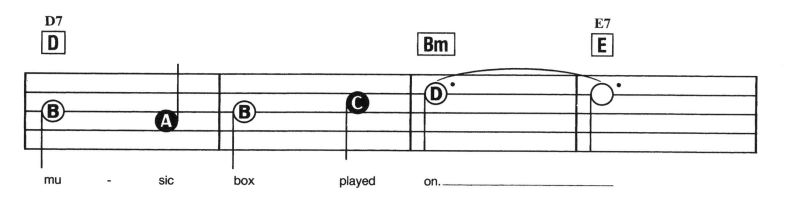

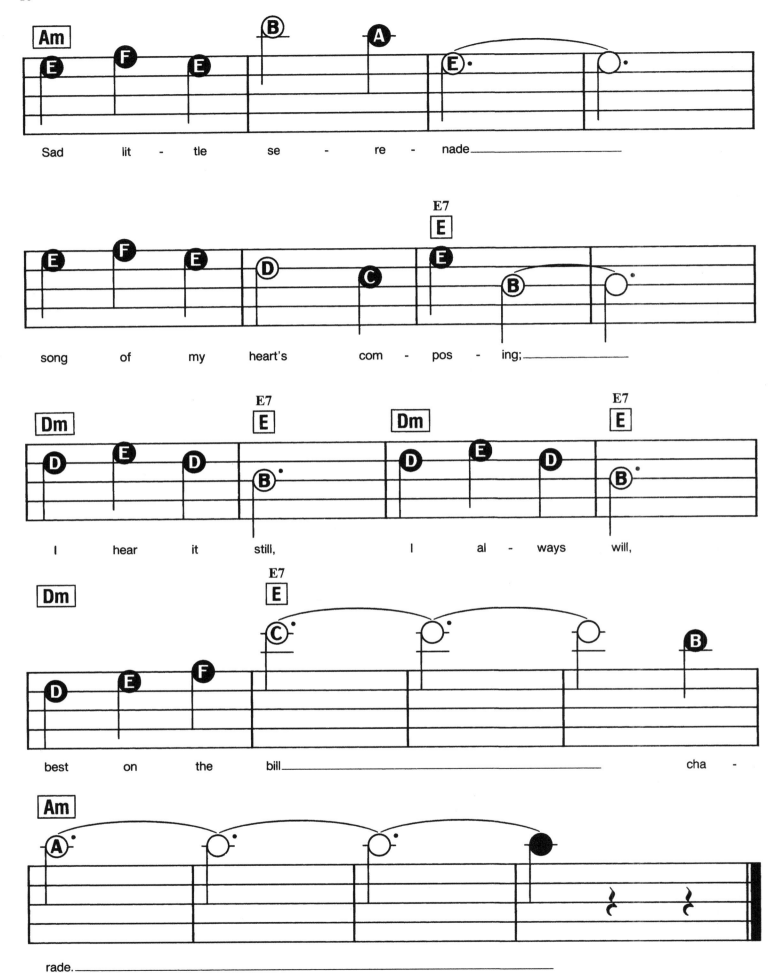

Darling Lili

Registration 2
Rhythm: Fox Trot or Swing

Words by Johnny Mercer
Music by Henry Mancini

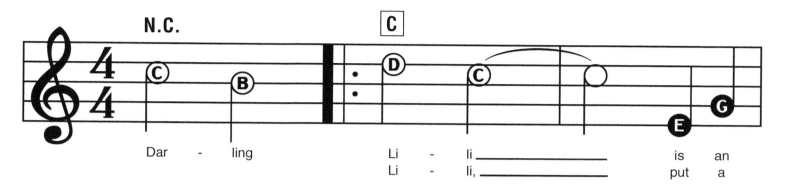

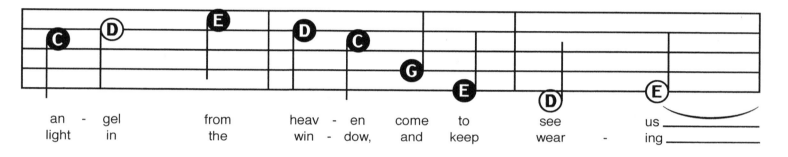

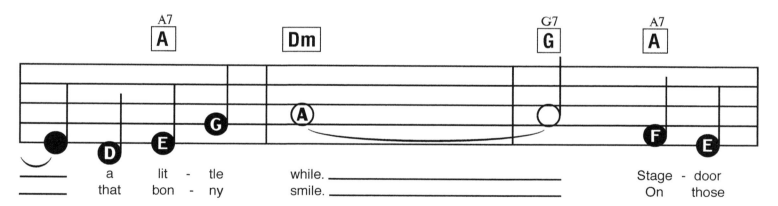

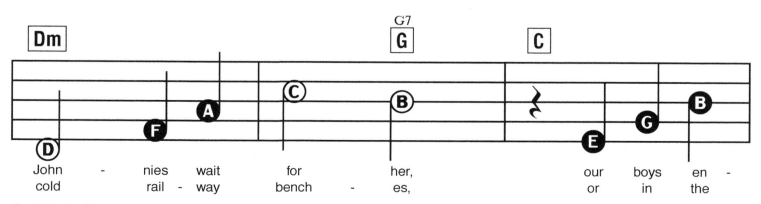

12

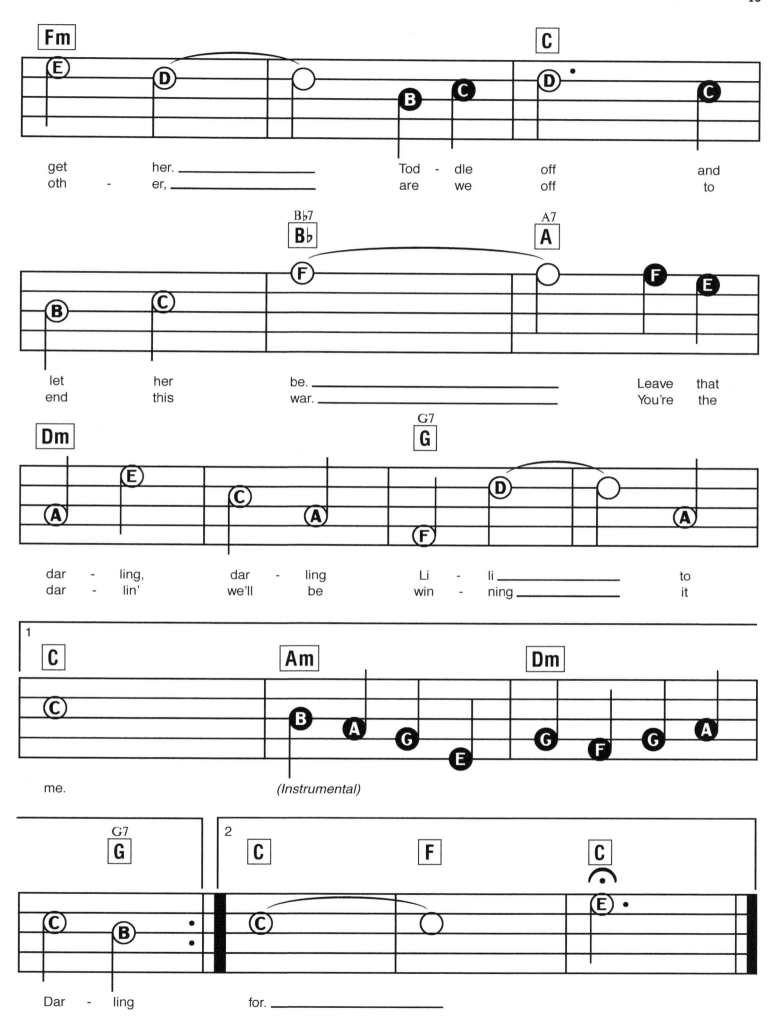

Crazy World
from VICTOR/VICTORIA

Registration 3
Rhythm: Waltz

Words by Leslie Bricusse
Music by Henry Mancini

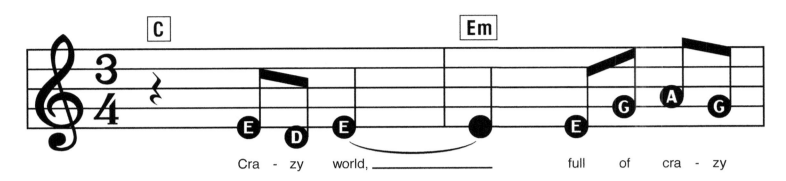

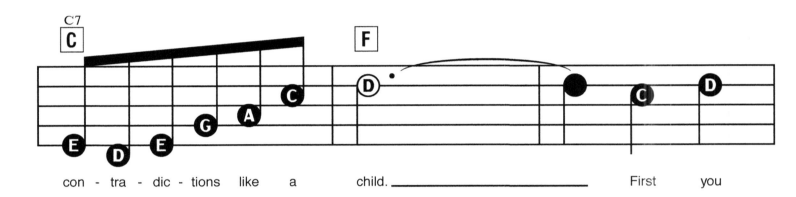

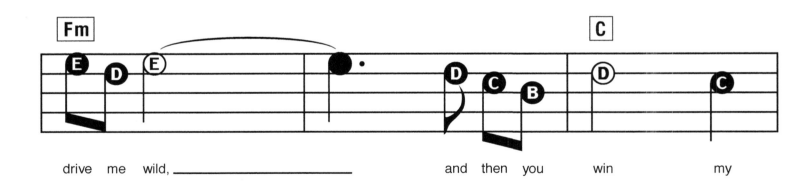

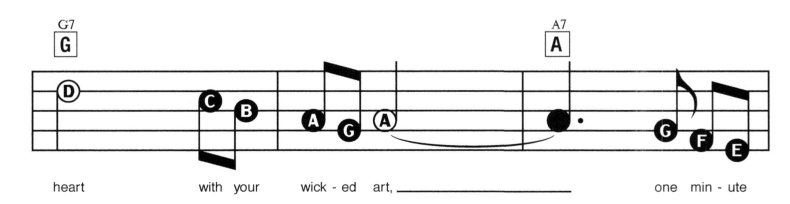

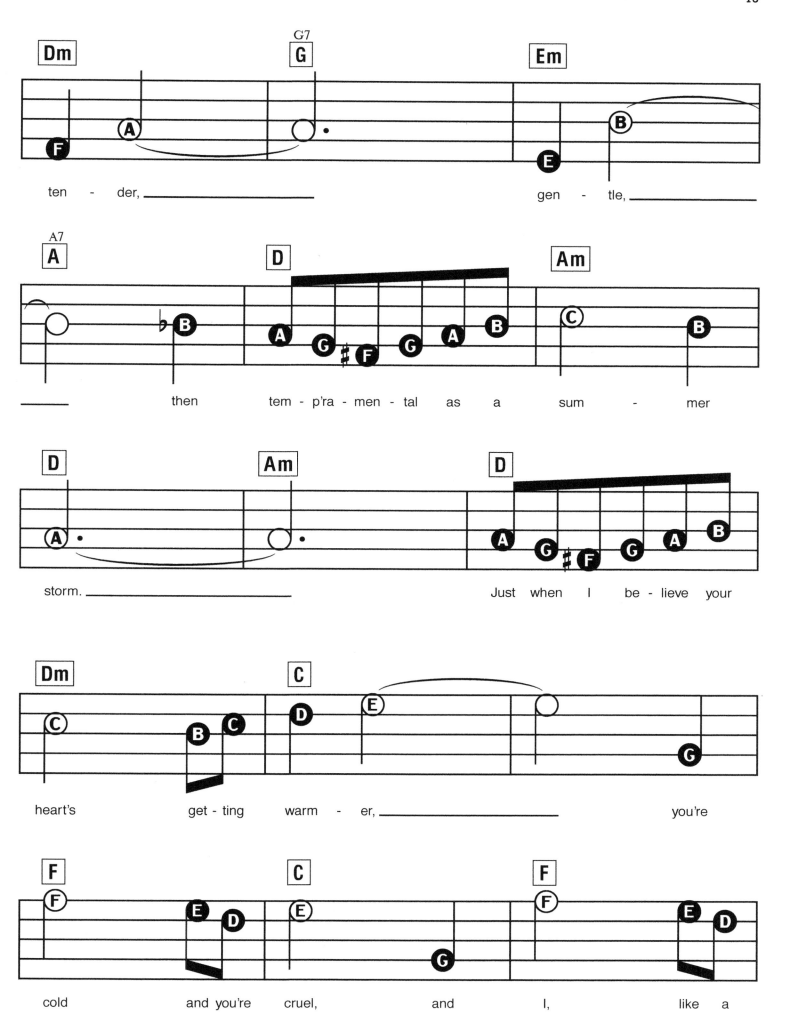

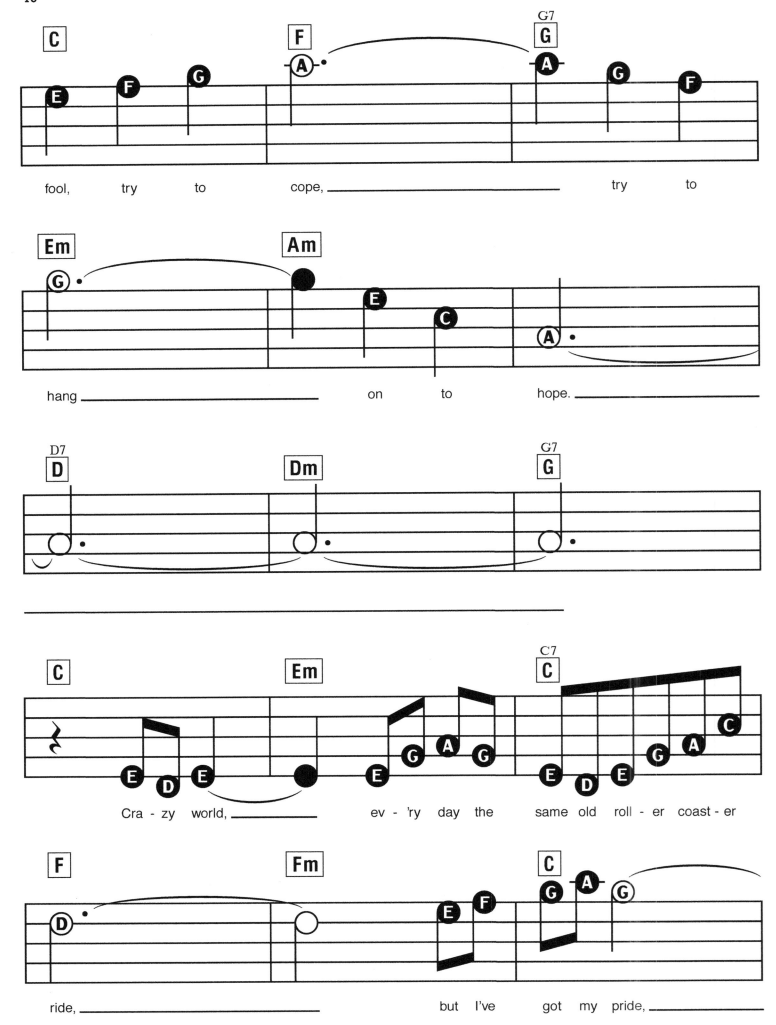

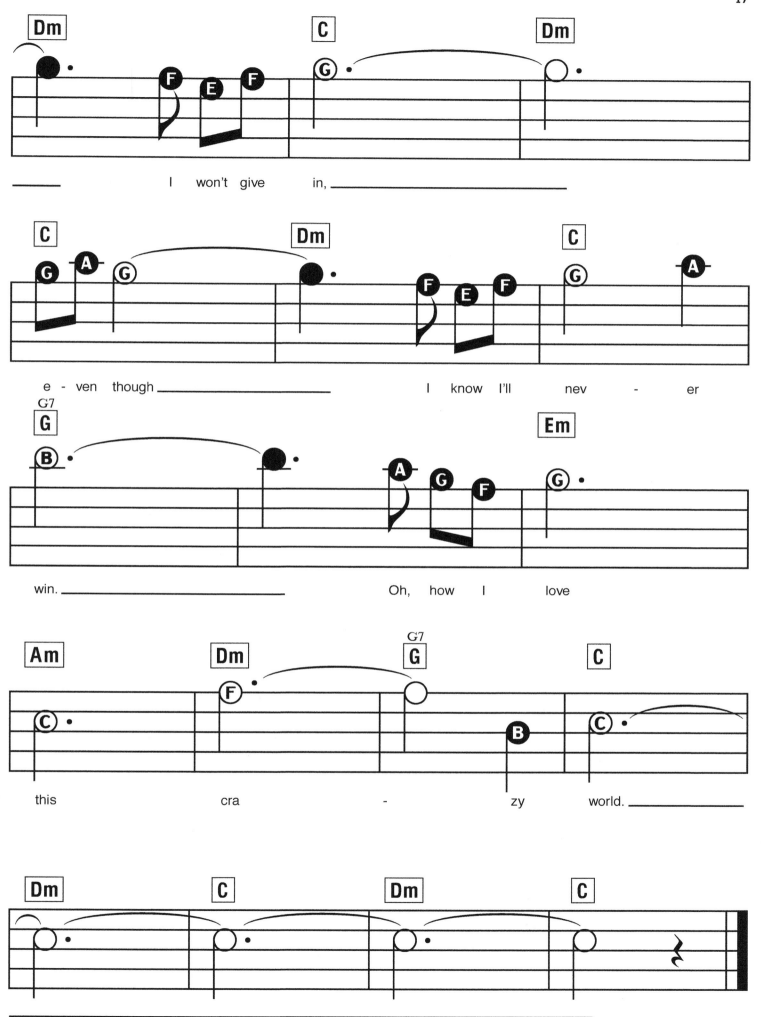

Days of Wine and Roses

from DAYS OF WINE AND ROSES

Registration 2
Rhythm: Swing or Ballad

Lyric by Johnny Mercer
Music by Henry Mancini

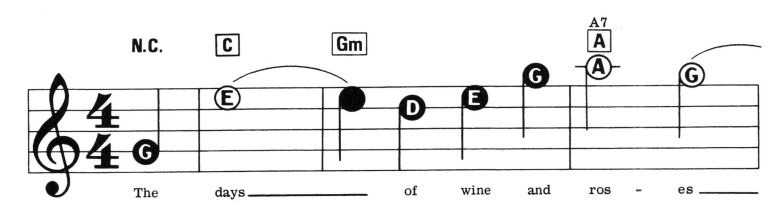

The days _____ of wine and ros - es _____

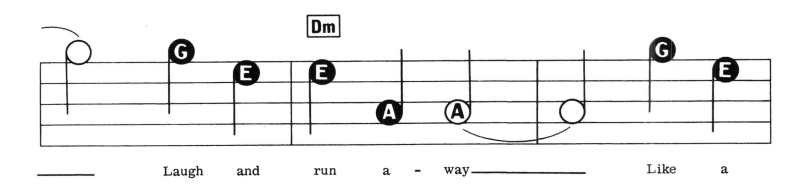

_____ Laugh and run a - way _____ Like a

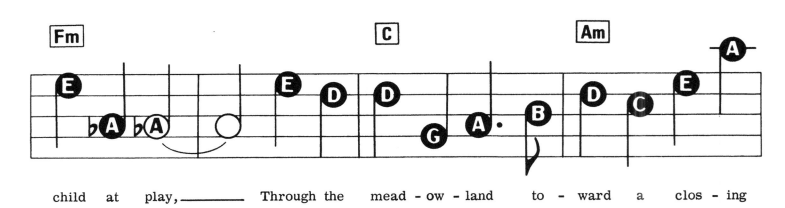

child at play, _____ Through the mead - ow - land to - ward a clos - ing

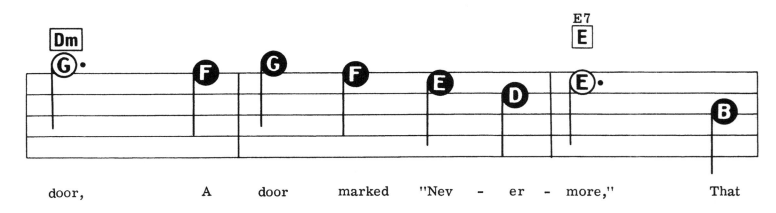

door, A door marked "Nev - er - more," That

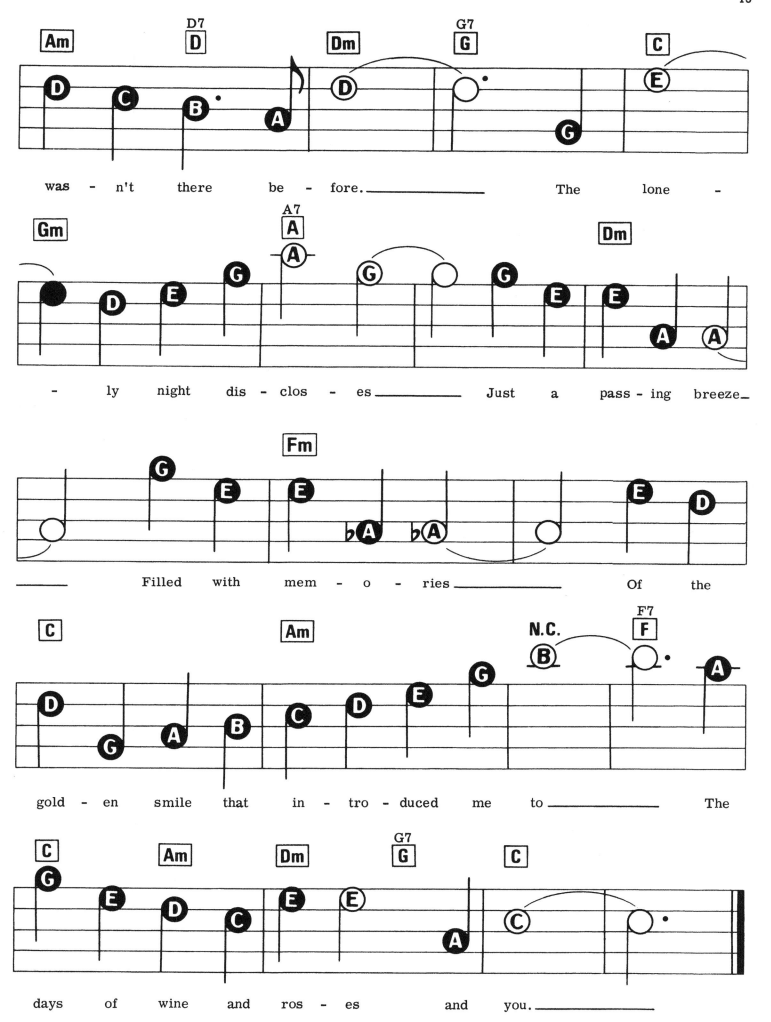

Dear Heart
from DEAR HEART

Registration 3
Rhythm: Waltz

Words by Jay Livingston and Ray Evans
Music by Henry Mancini

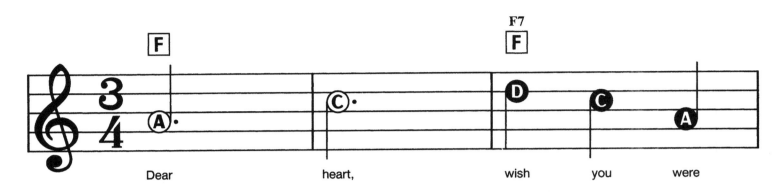

Dear — heart, — wish you were

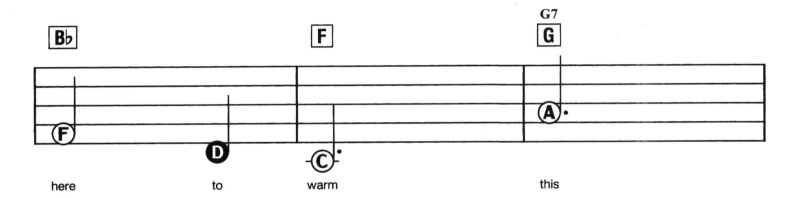

here — to warm — this

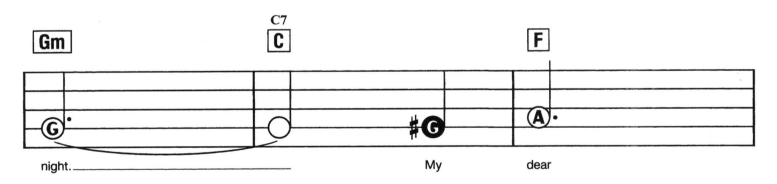

night. — My dear

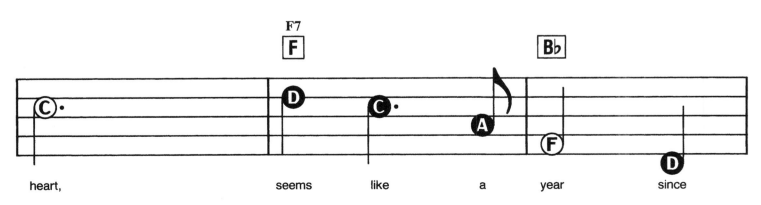

heart, — seems like a year since

21

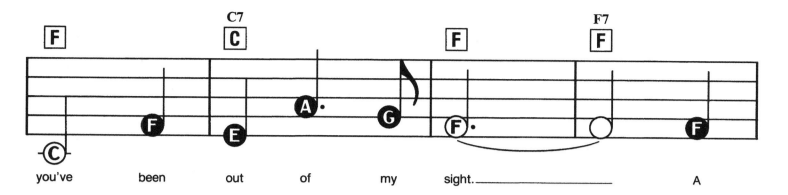

you've been out of my sight._____ A

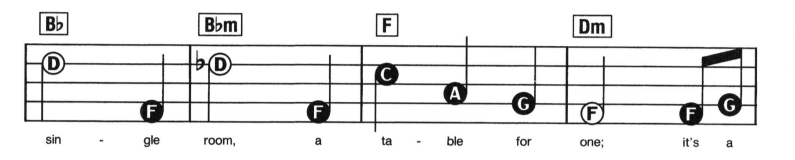

sin - gle room, a ta - ble for one; it's a

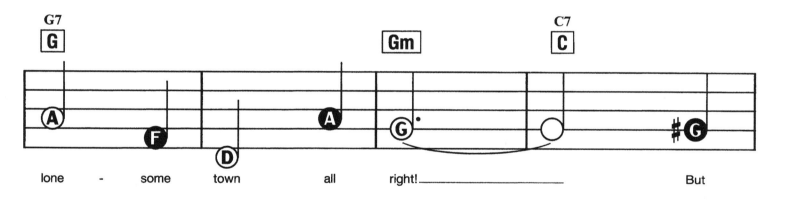

lone - some town all right!_____ But

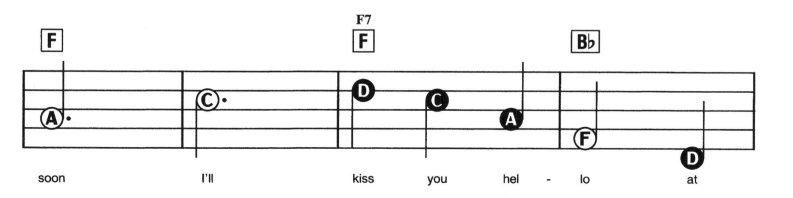

soon I'll kiss you hel - lo at

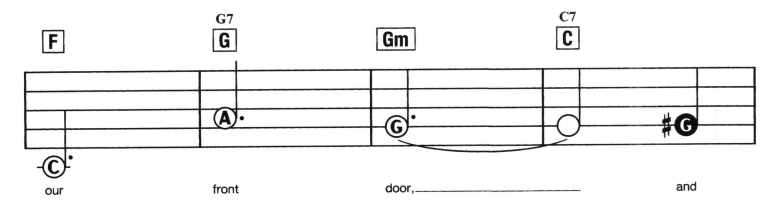

our   front   door,_____ and

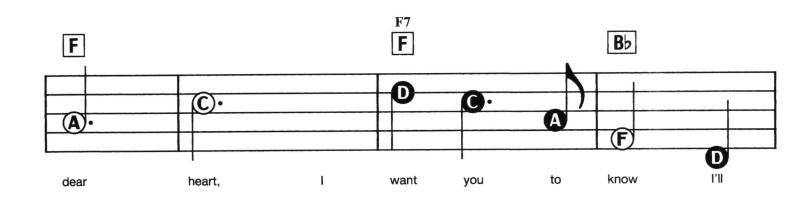

dear   heart,   I want you to know I'll

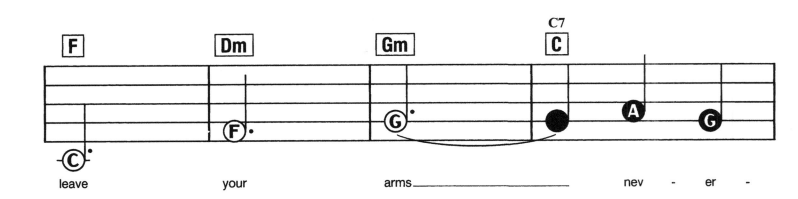

leave   your   arms_____ nev - er -

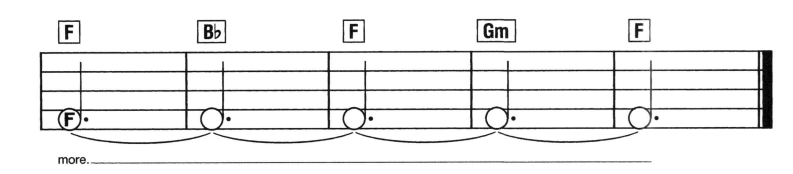

more._____

Theme from Hatari

Registration 1
Rhythm: None

By Henry Mancini

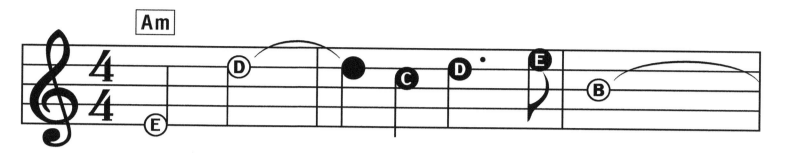

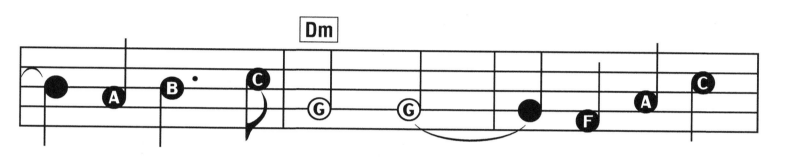

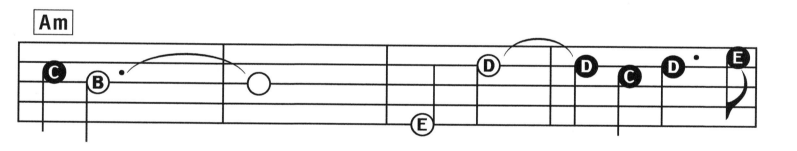

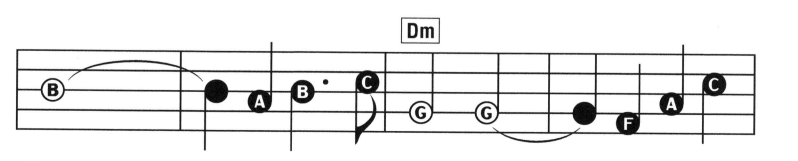

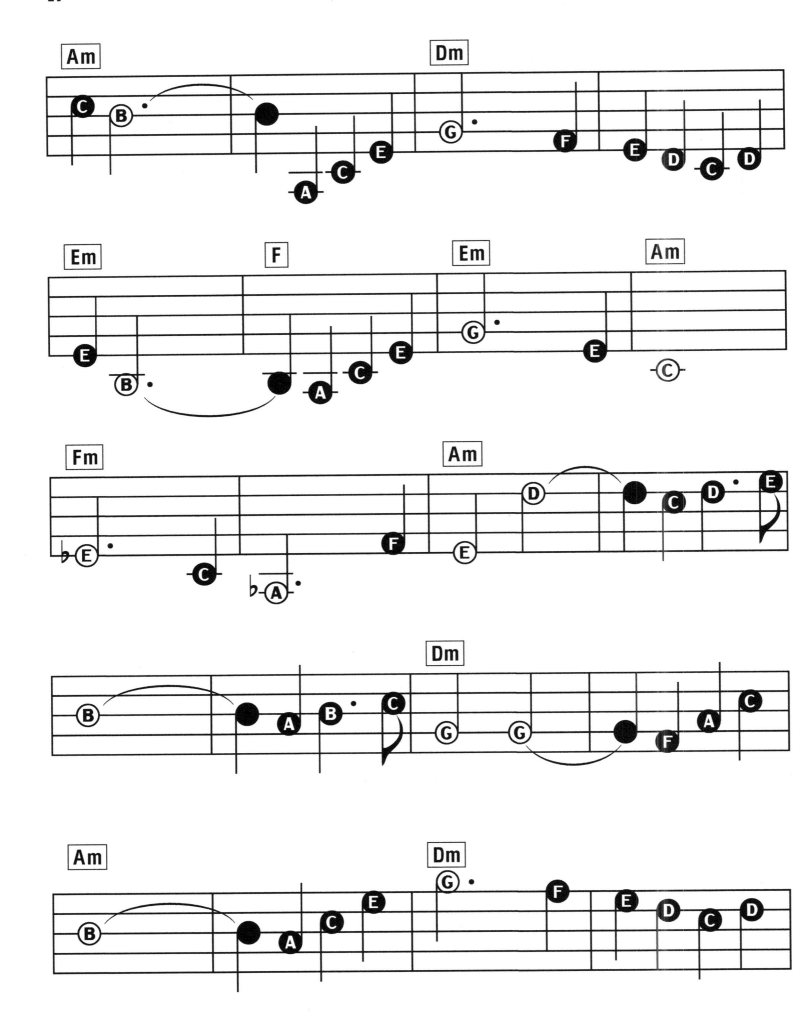

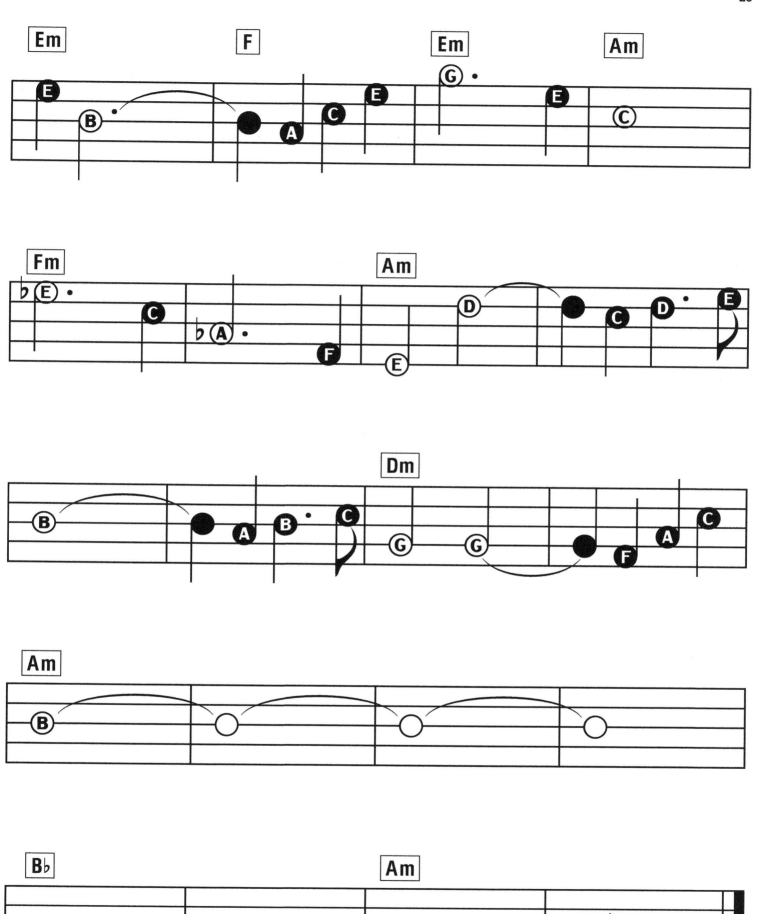

25

Dreamsville

Registration 2
Rhythm: Fox Trot or Swing

Lyrics by Jay Livingston and Ray Evans
Music by Henry Mancini

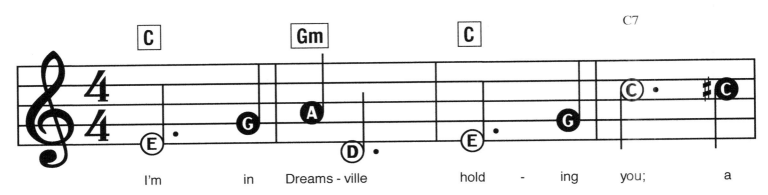

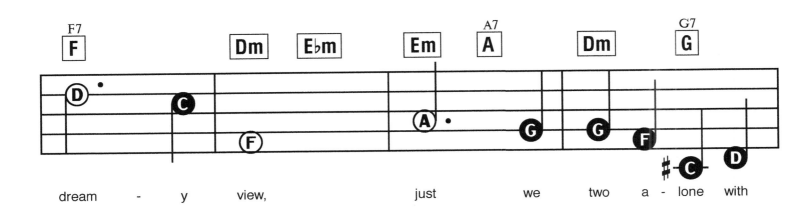

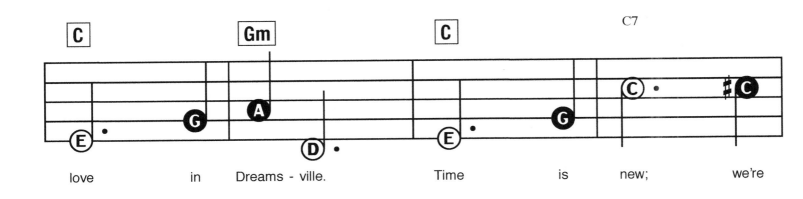

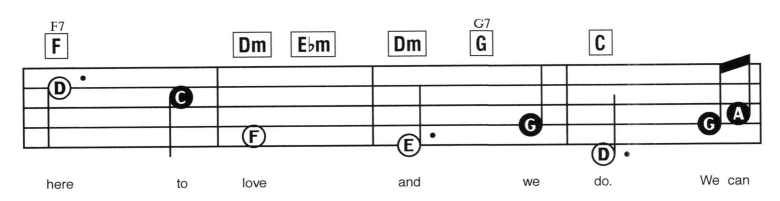

27

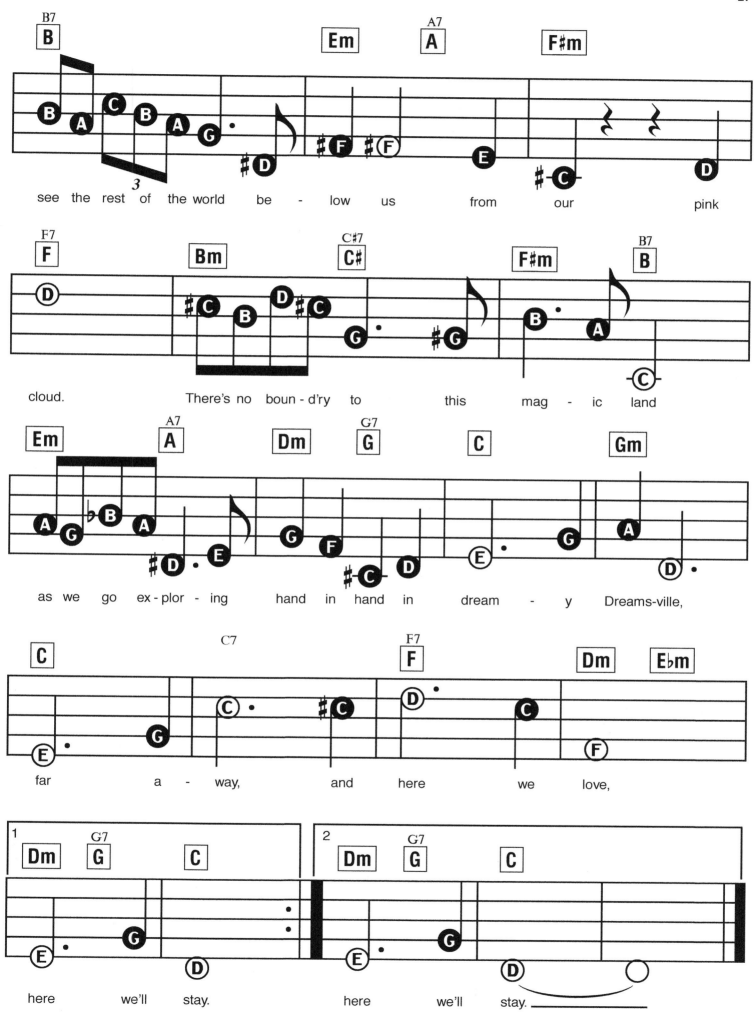

How Soon

Registration 8
Rhythm: Ballad or Fox Trot

Words by Al Stillman
Music by Henry Mancini

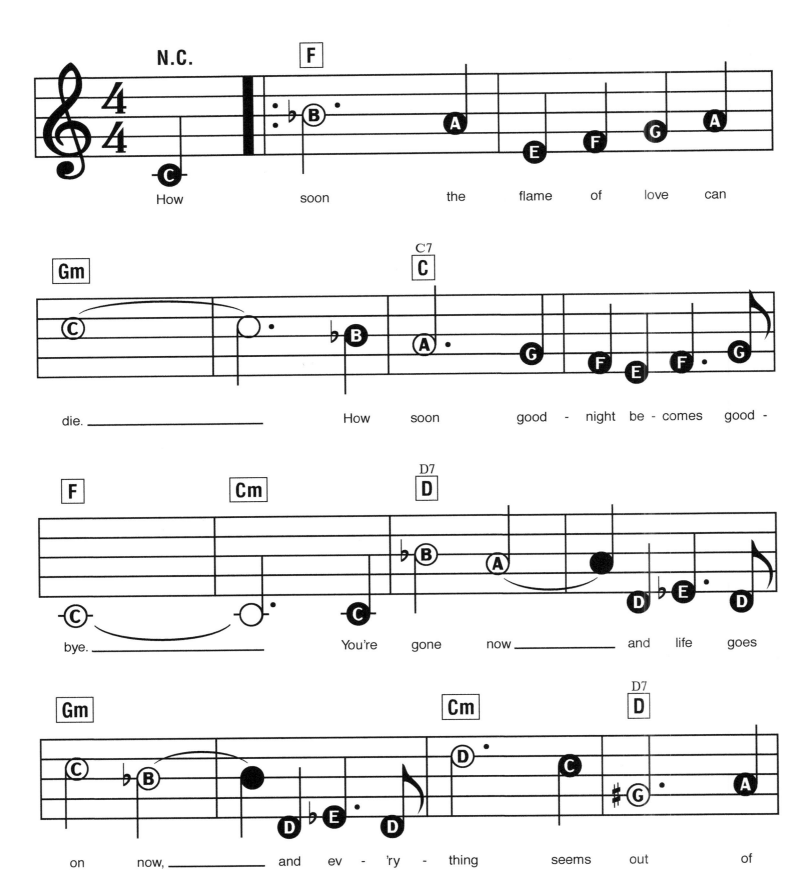

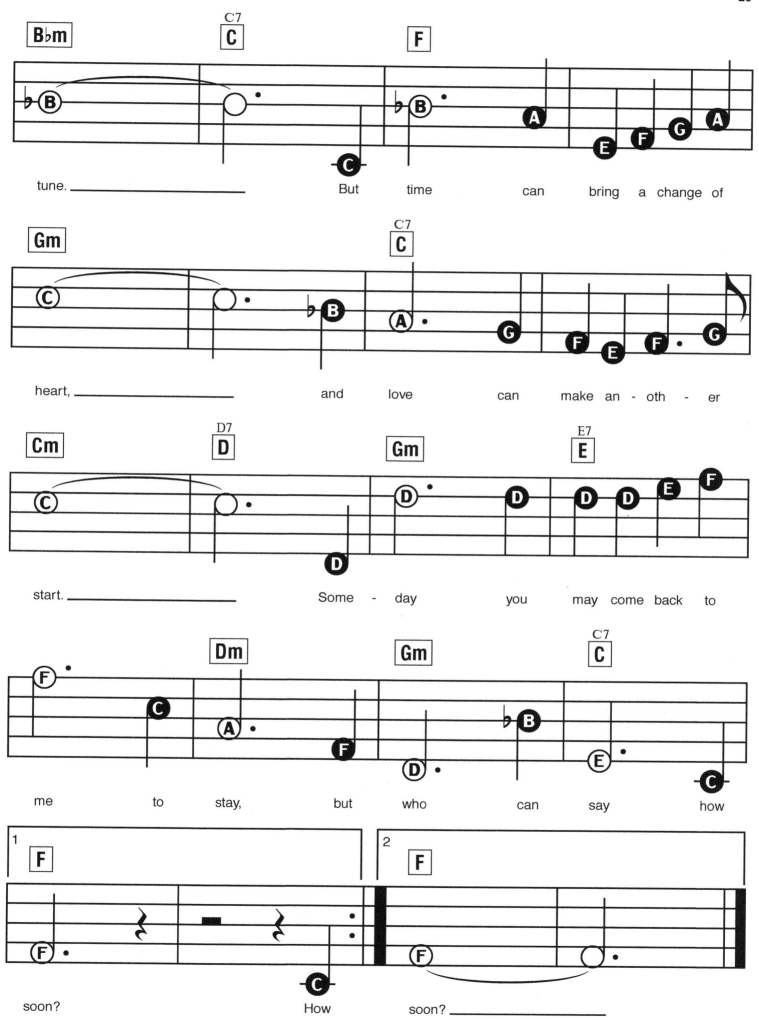

In the Arms of Love

Registration 1
Rhythm: Ballad or Fox Trot

Words by Ray Evans and Jay Livingston
Music by Henry Mancini

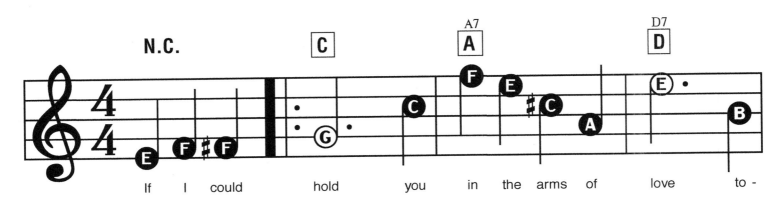

If I could hold you in the arms of love to-

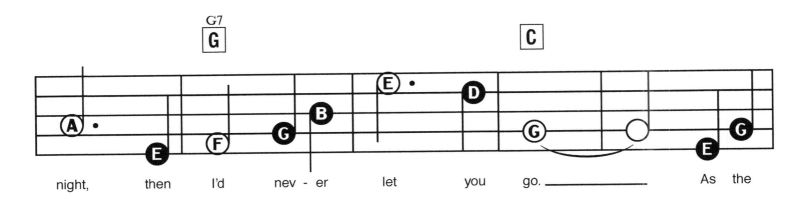

night, then I'd nev - er let you go. _____ As the

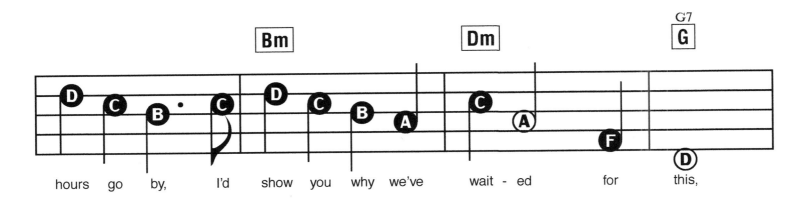

hours go by, I'd show you why we've wait - ed for this,

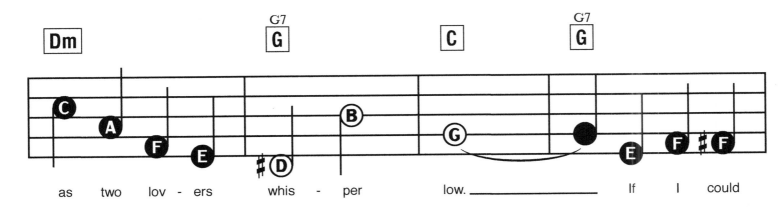

as two lov - ers whis - per low. _____ If I could

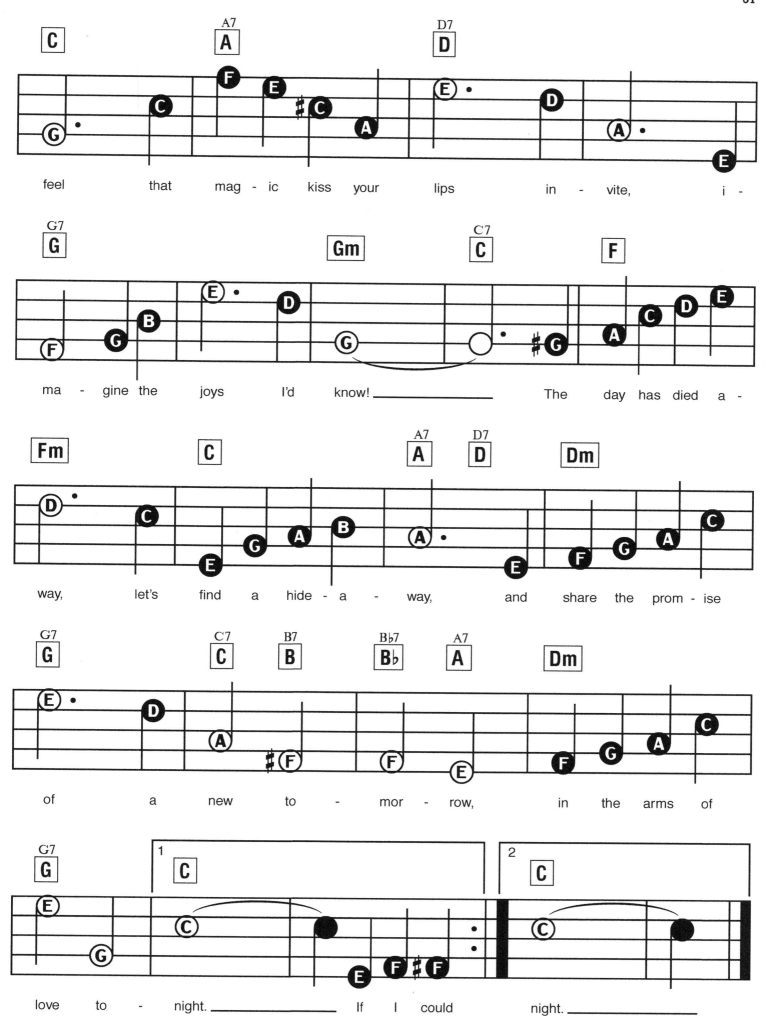

Life in a Looking Glass

Registration 8
Rhythm: Ballad or Fox Trot

Lyrics by Leslie Bricusse
Music by Henry Mancini

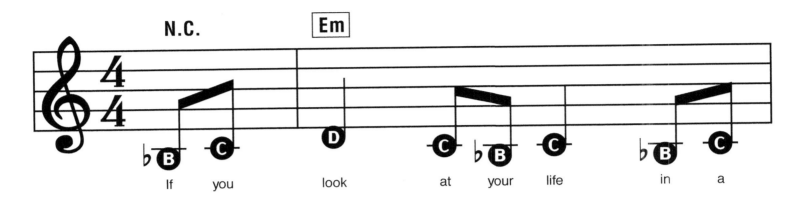

If you look at your life in a

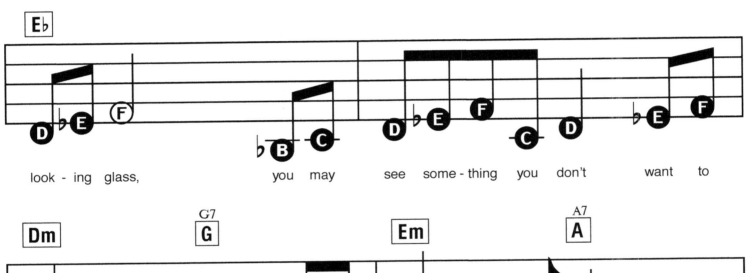

look - ing glass, you may see some - thing you don't want to

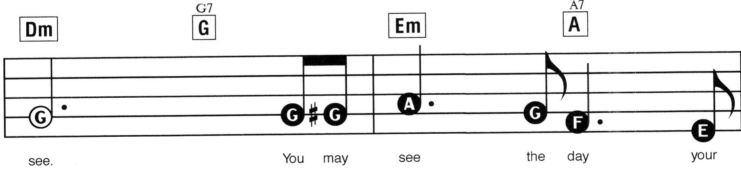

see. You may see the day your

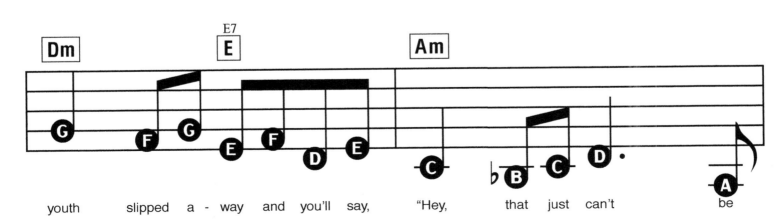

youth slipped a - way and you'll say, "Hey, that just can't be

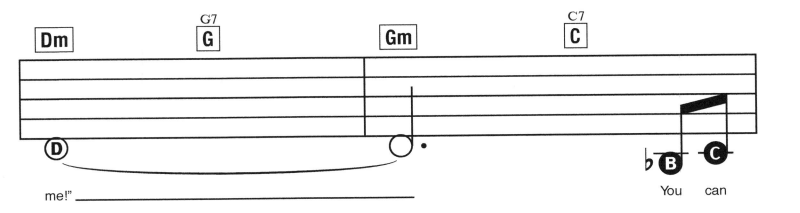

Dm | G7 / G | Gm | C7 / C

me!" _____ You can

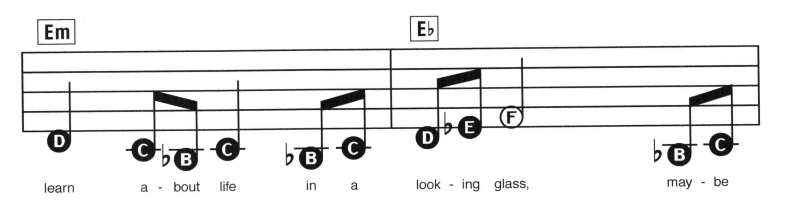

Em | Eb

learn a - bout life in a look - ing glass, may - be

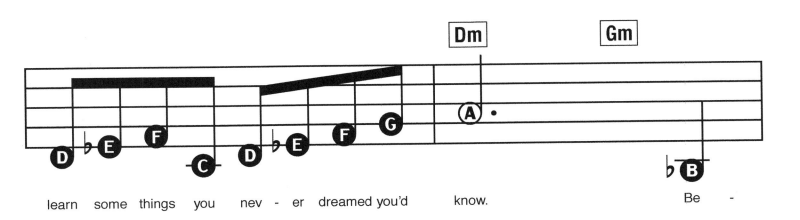

Dm | Gm

learn some things you nev - er dreamed you'd know. Be -

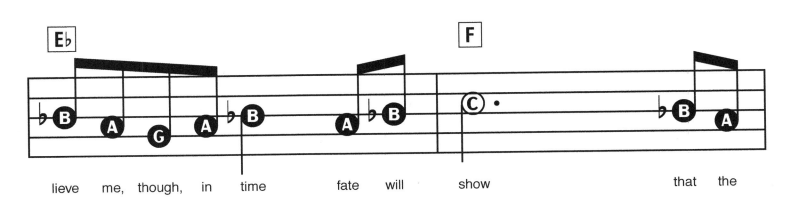

Eb | F

lieve me, though, in time fate will show that the

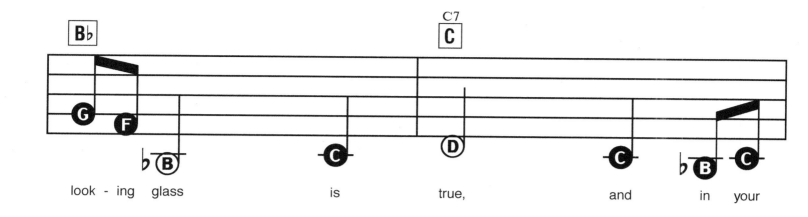

look - ing glass   is   true,   and   in   your

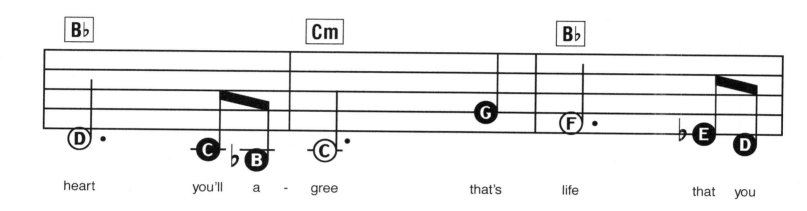

heart   you'll   a - gree   that's   life   that   you

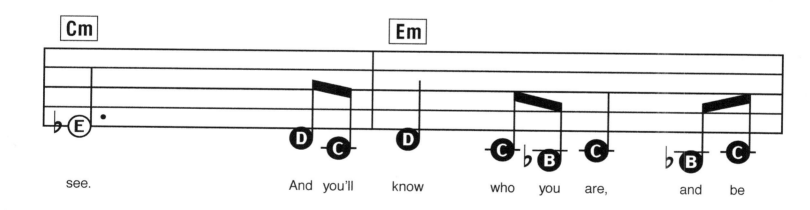

see.   And   you'll   know   who   you   are,   and   be

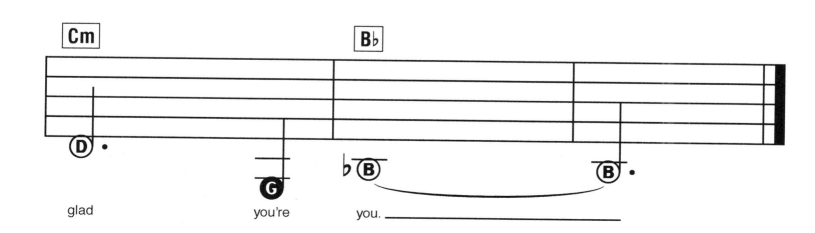

glad   you're   you. _____

Moment to Moment

Registration 3
Rhythm: Ballad or Fox Trot

Words by Johnny Mercer
Music by Henry Mancini

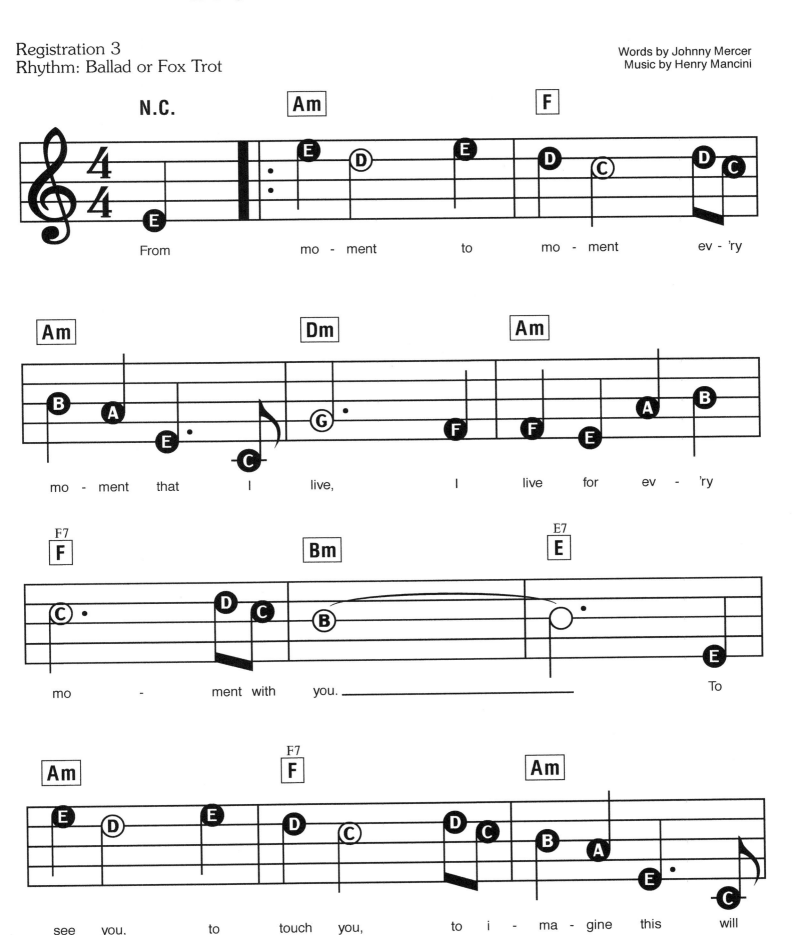

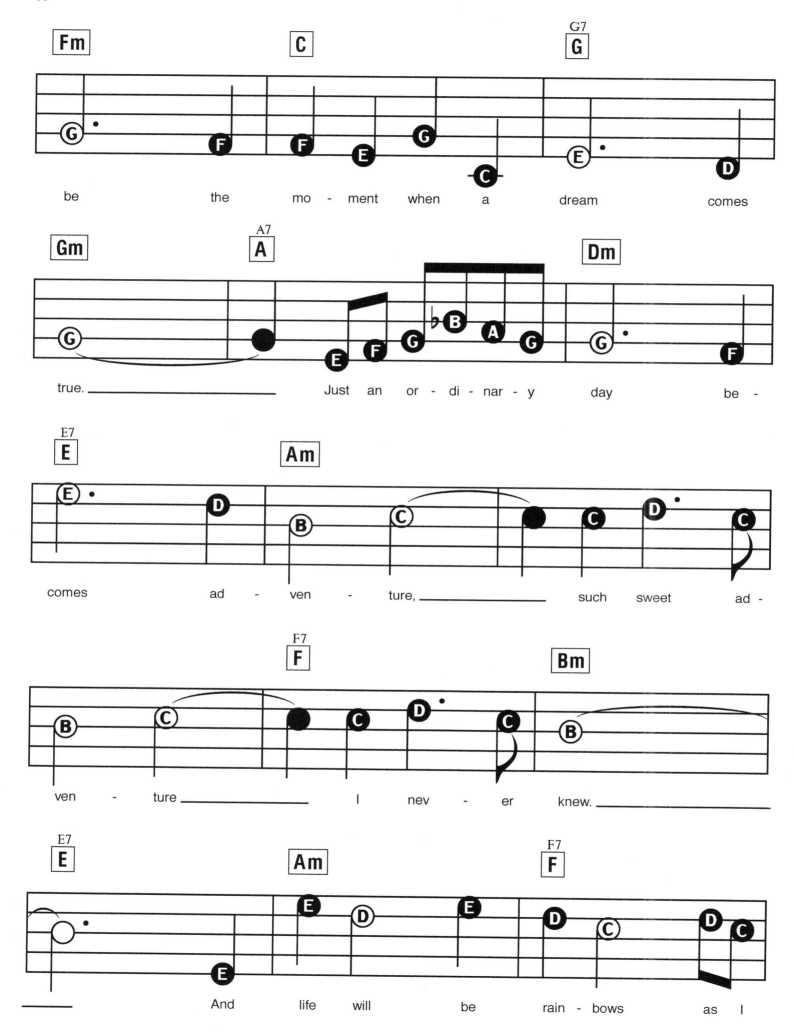

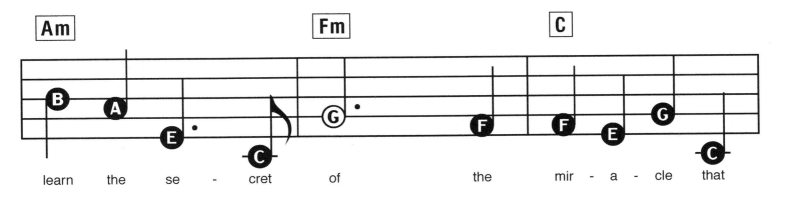

learn the se - cret of the mir - a - cle that

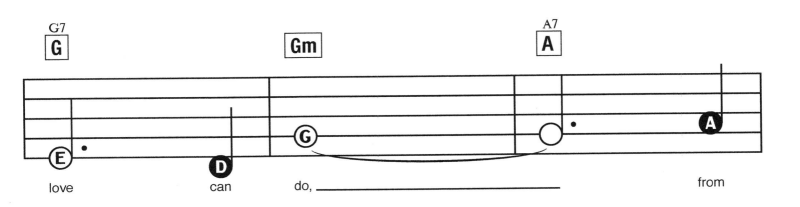

love can do, _____ from

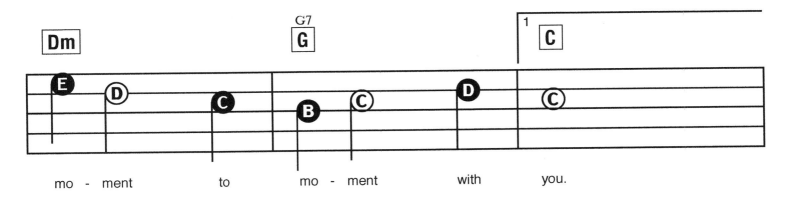

mo - ment to mo - ment with you.

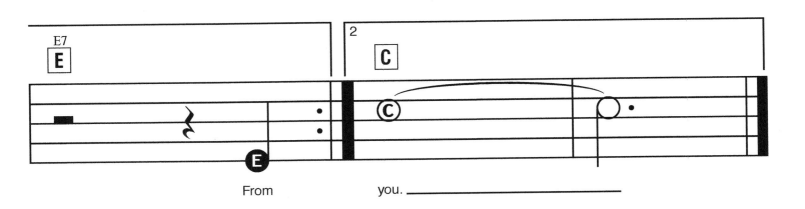

From you. _____

Mr. Lucky

Registration 8
Rhythm: Swing

Lyrics by Jay Livingston and Ray Evans
Music by Henry Mancini

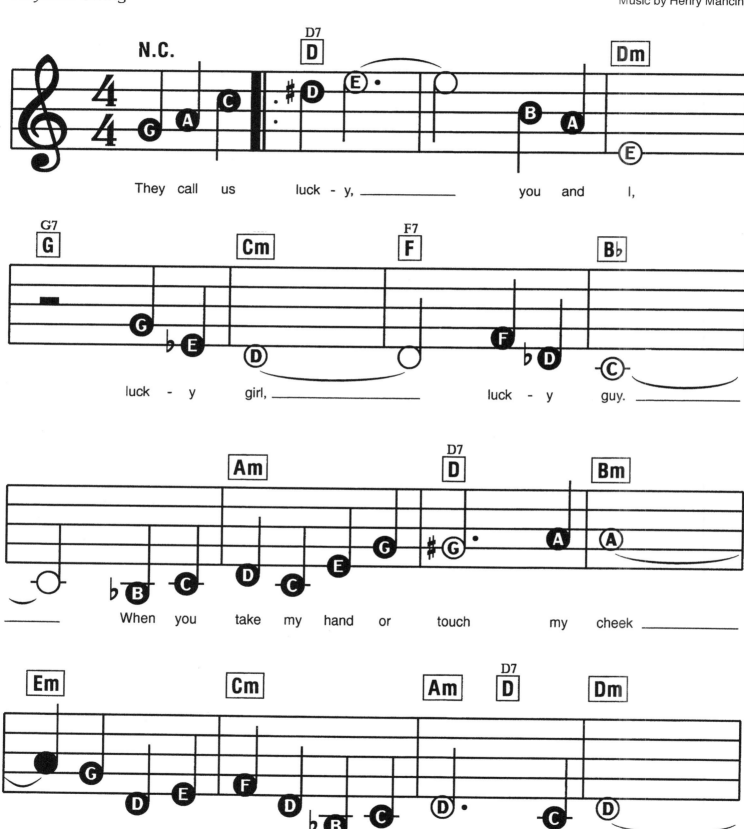

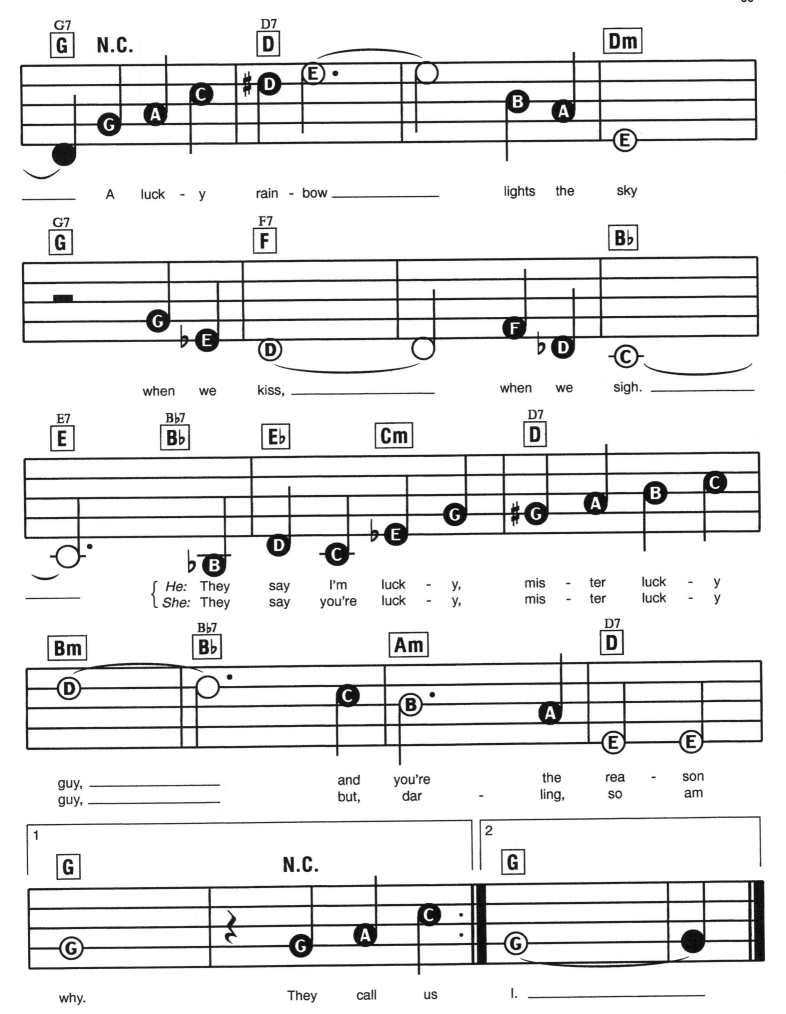

Moon River
from the Paramount Picture BREAKFAST AT TIFFANY'S

Registration 3
Rhythm: Waltz

Words by Johnny Mercer
Music by Henry Mancini

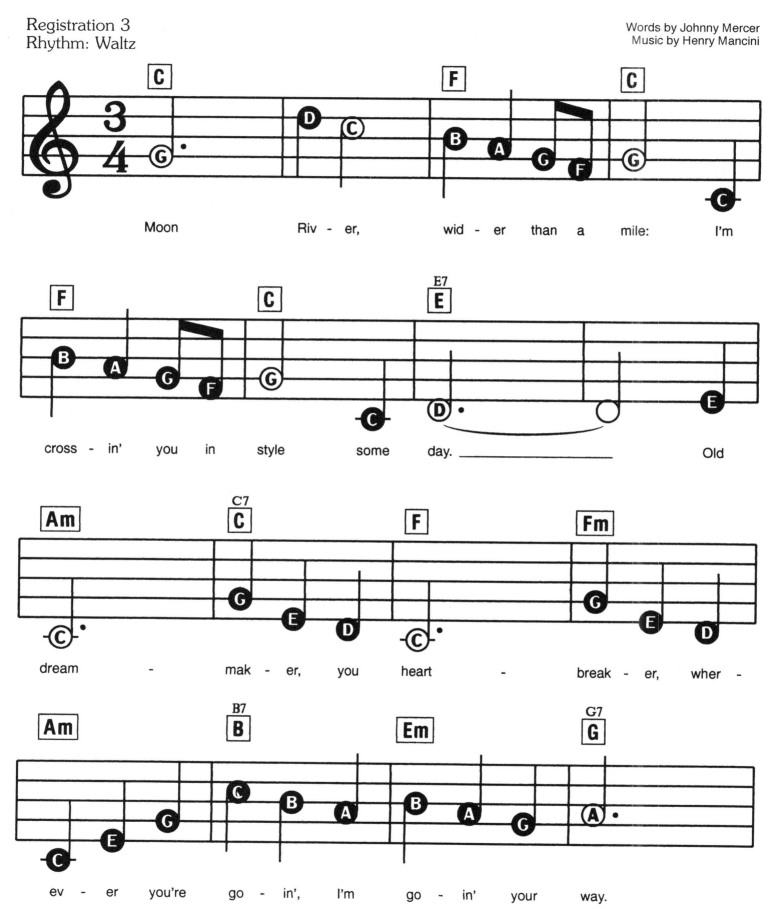

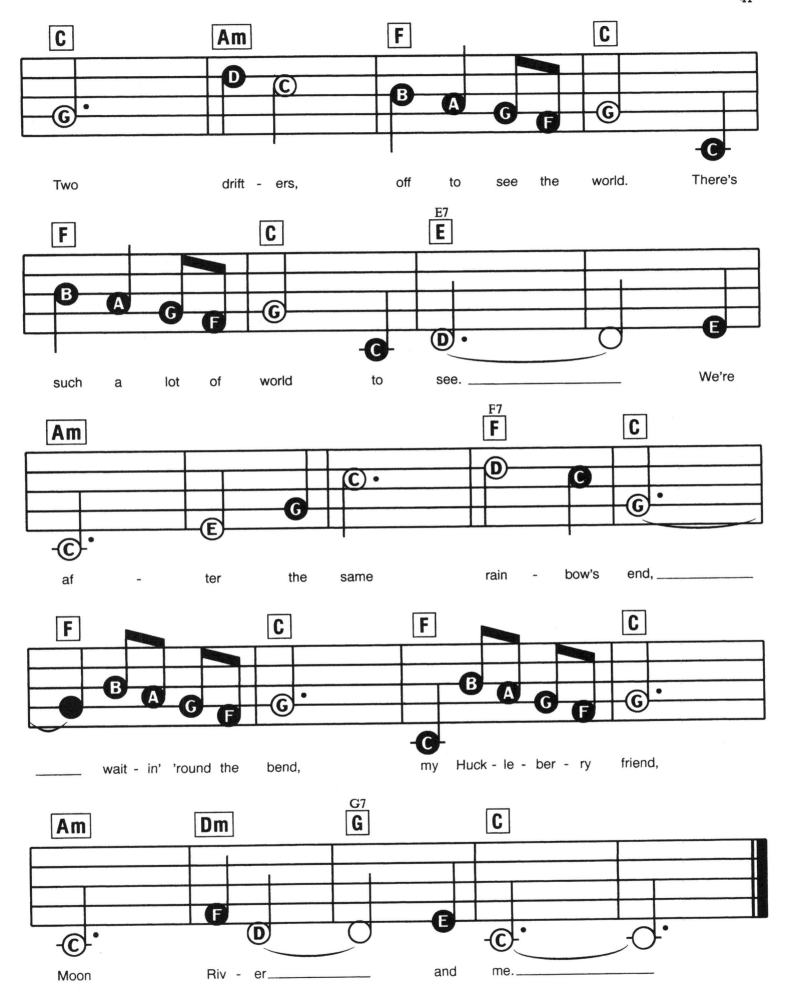

Peter Gunn
Theme Song from the Television Series

Registration 5
Rhythm: Rock or 8-Beat

By Henry Mancini

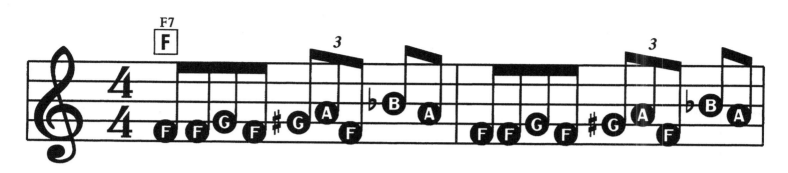

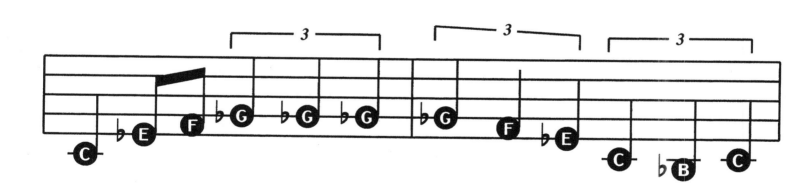

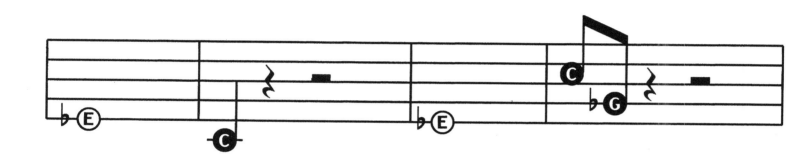

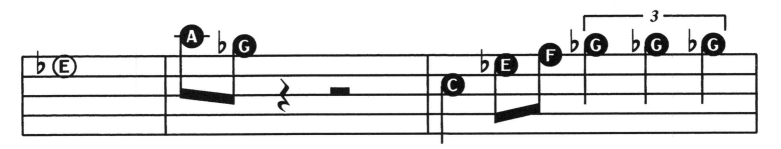

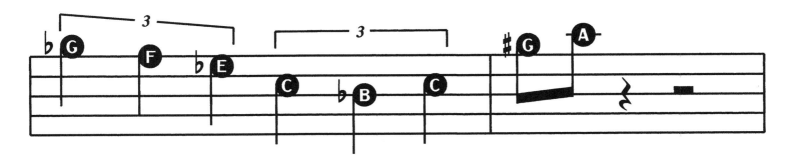

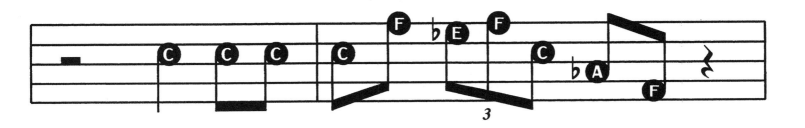

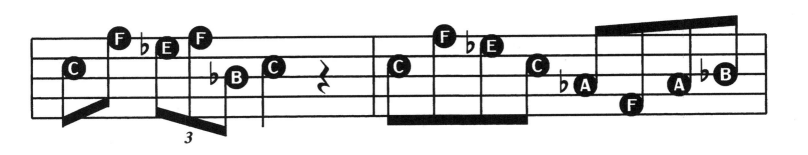

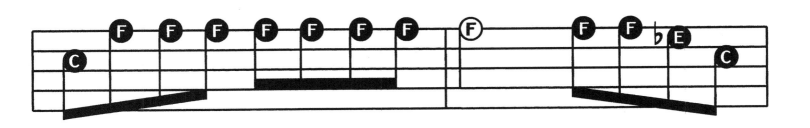

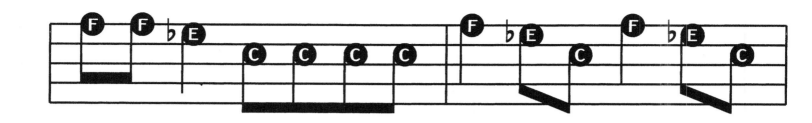

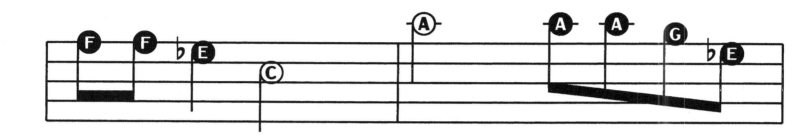

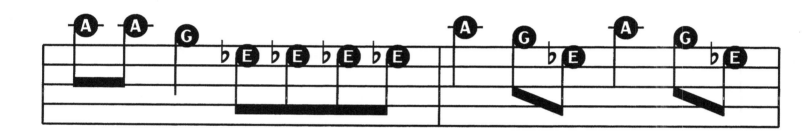

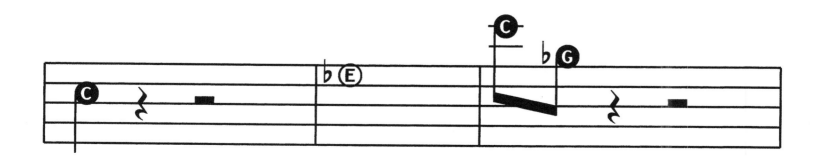

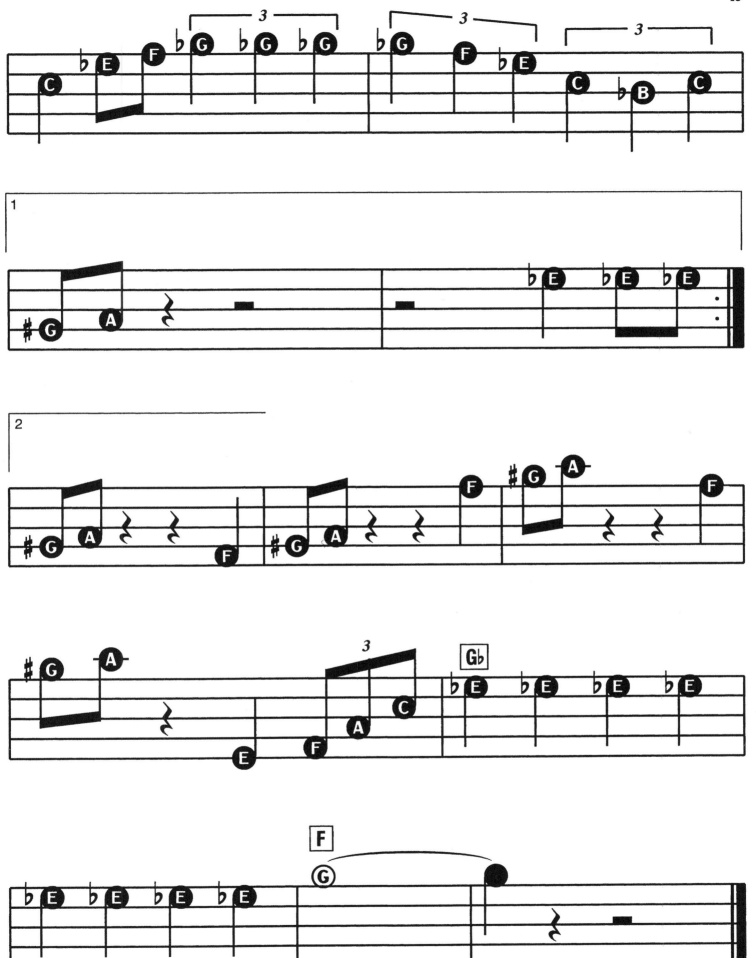

The Pink Panther
from THE PINK PANTHER

Registration 7
Rhythm: Swing

By Henry Mancini

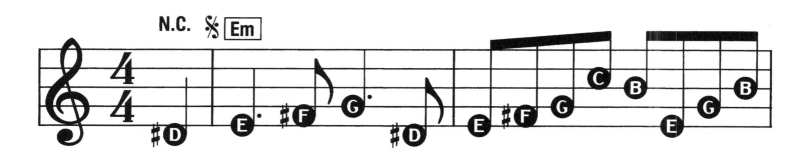

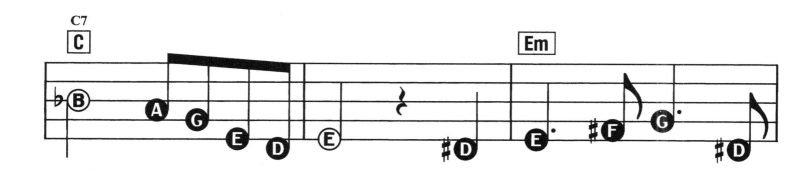

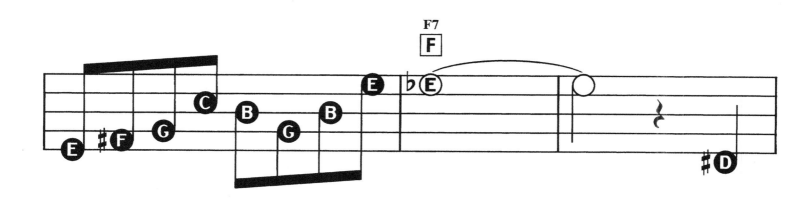

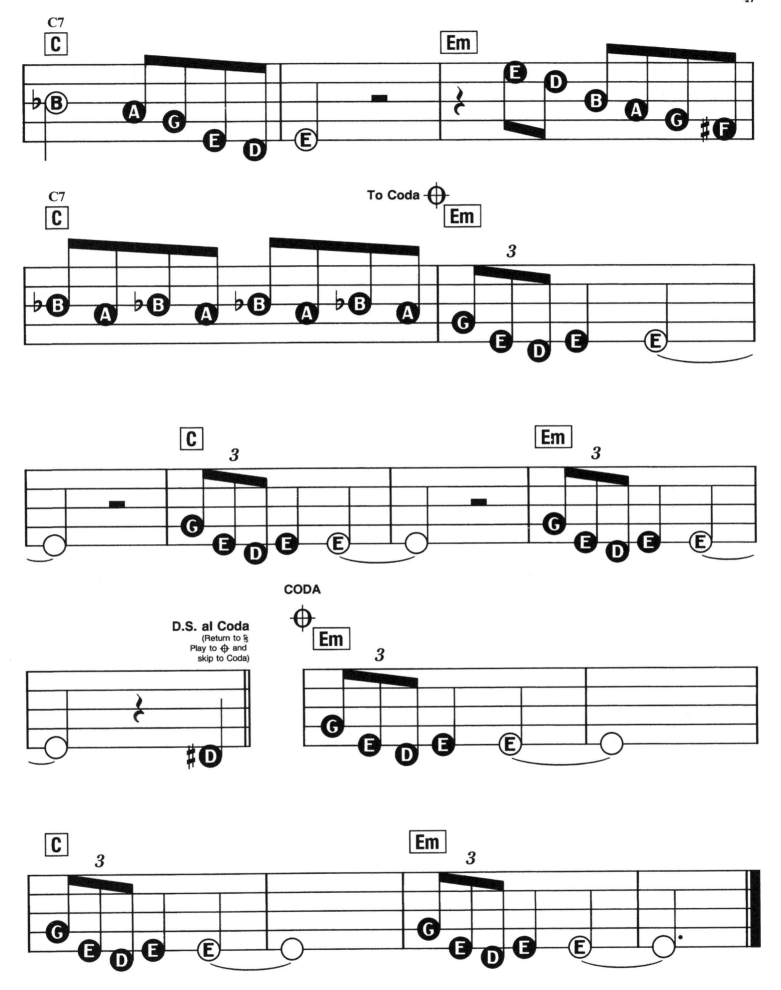

A Shot in the Dark

from the Motion Picture A SHOT IN THE DARK

Registration 4
Rhythm: Swing

Words by Leslie Bricusse
Music by Henry Mancini

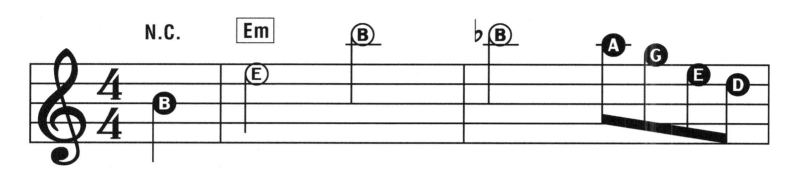

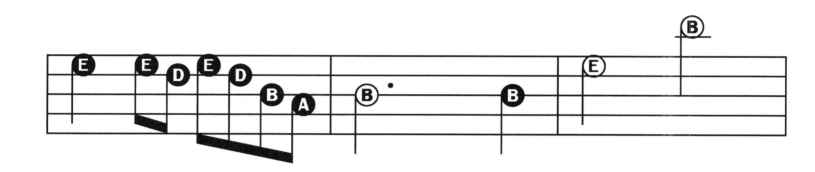

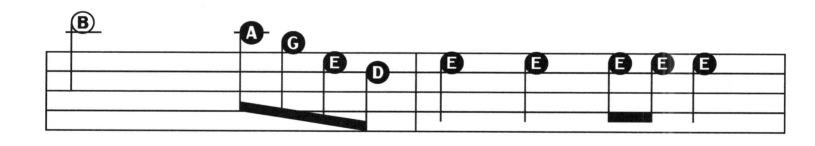

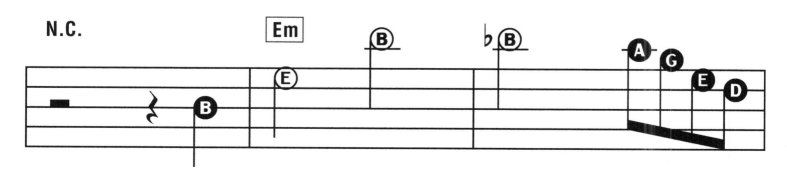

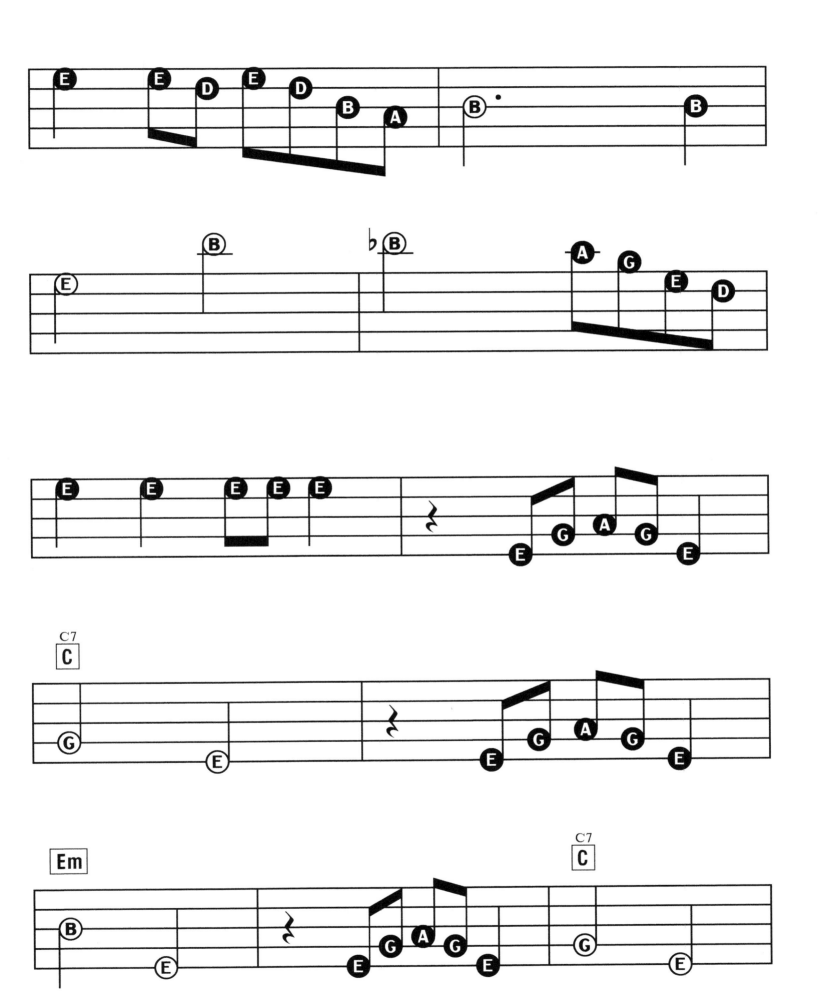

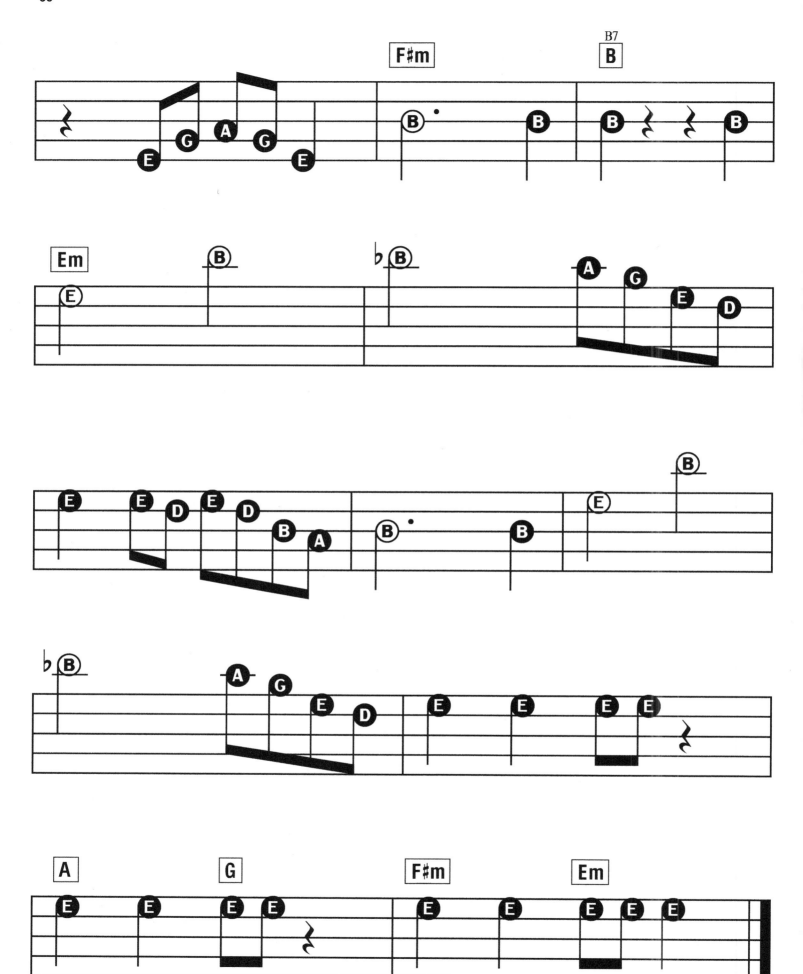

The Thorn Birds
(Main Theme)

Registration 3
Rhythm: Waltz

By Henry Mancini

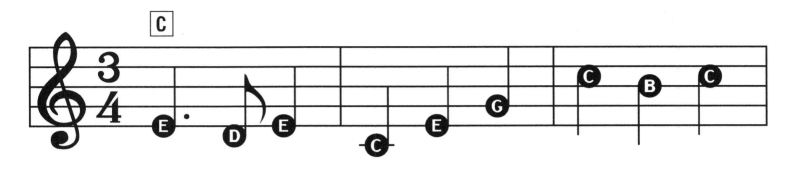

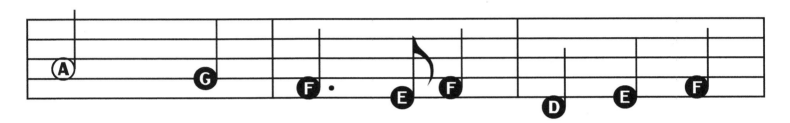

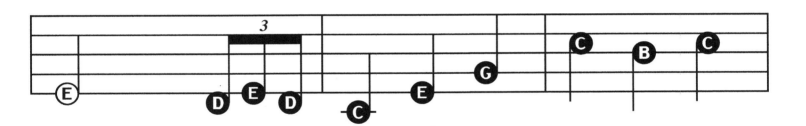

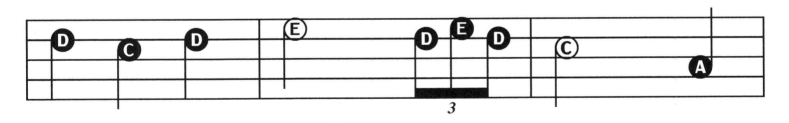

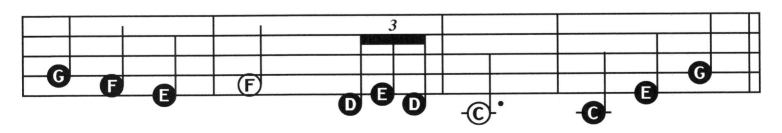

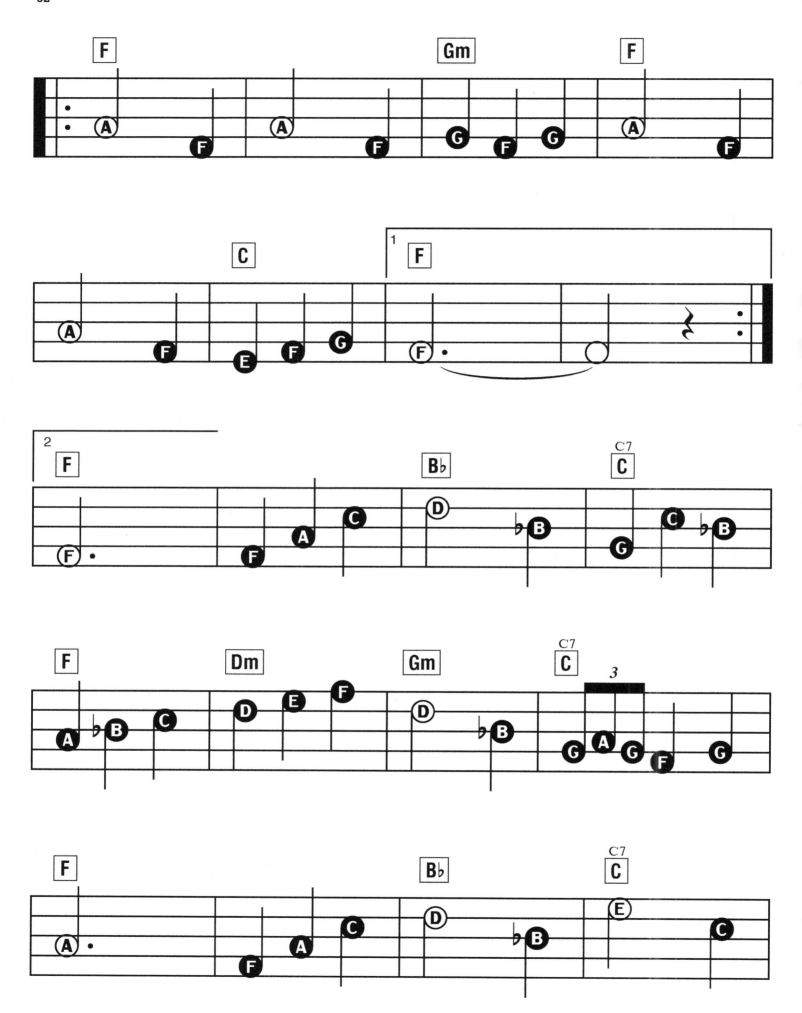

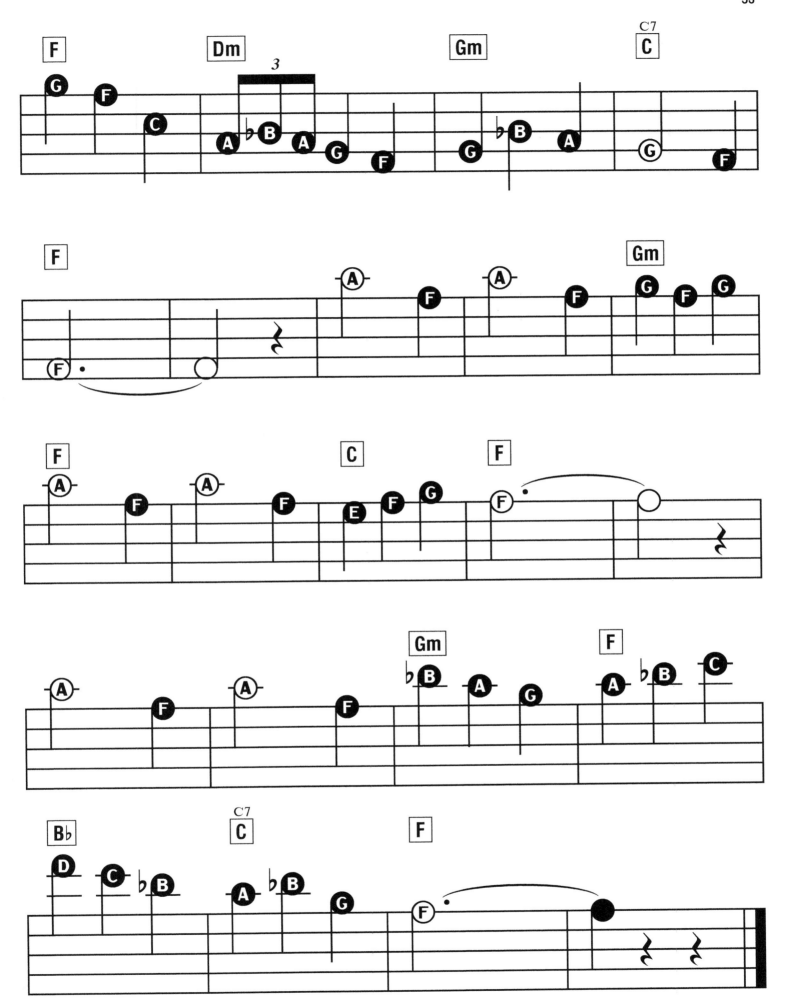

The Sweetheart Tree
from THE GREAT RACE

Registration 2
Rhythm: Waltz

Words by Johnny Mercer
Music by Henry Mancini

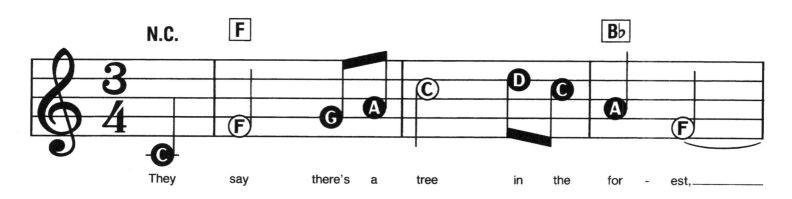

They say there's a tree in the for - est,

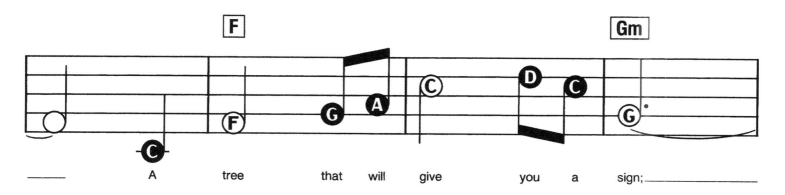

A tree that will give you a sign;

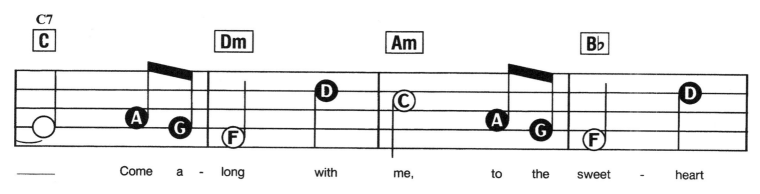

Come a - long with me, to the sweet - heart

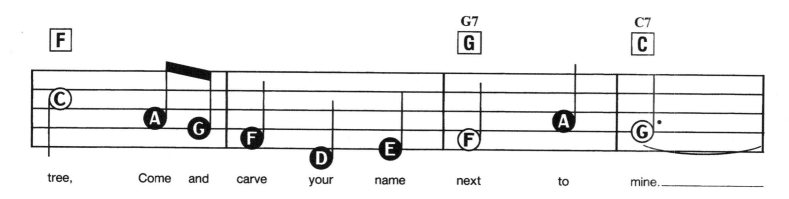

tree, Come and carve your name next to mine.

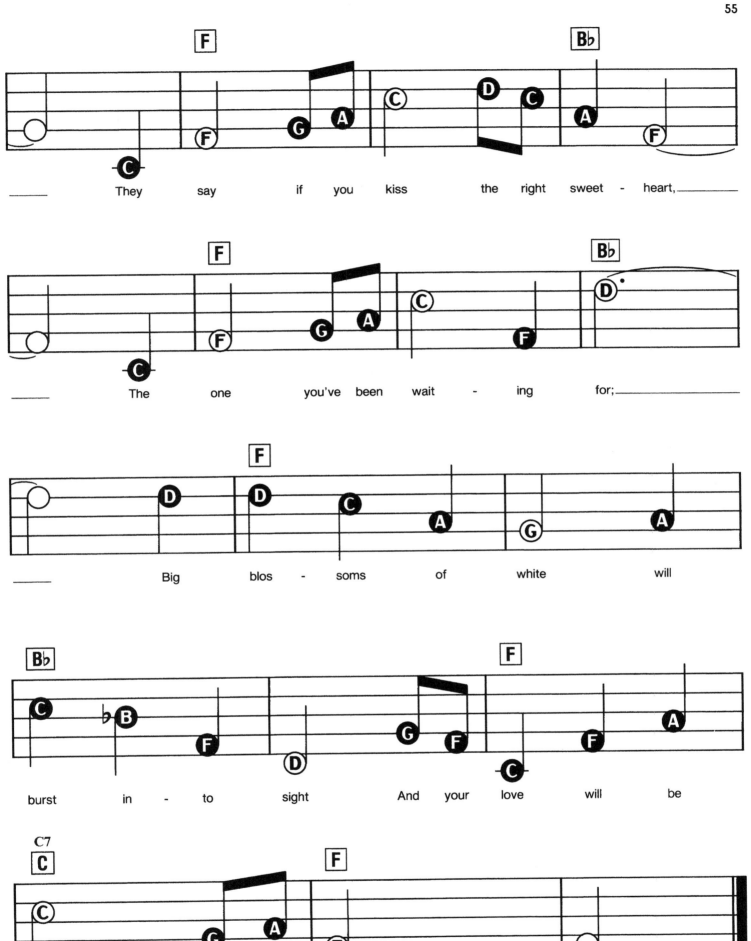

Two for the Road

Registration 8
Rhythm: Bossa Nova or Latin

Music by Henry Mancini
Words by Leslie Bricusse

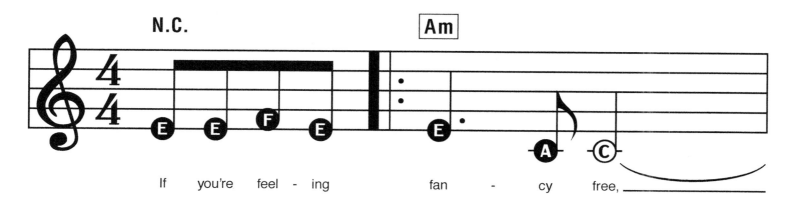

If you're feel - ing fan - cy free, _____

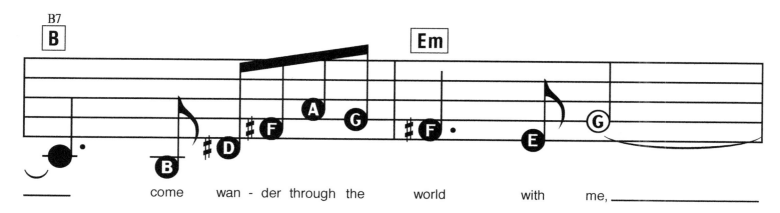

_____ come wan - der through the world with me, _____

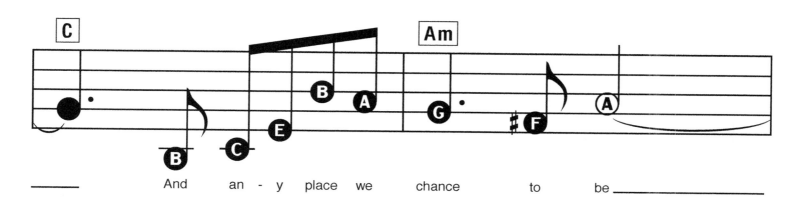

_____ And an - y place we chance to be _____

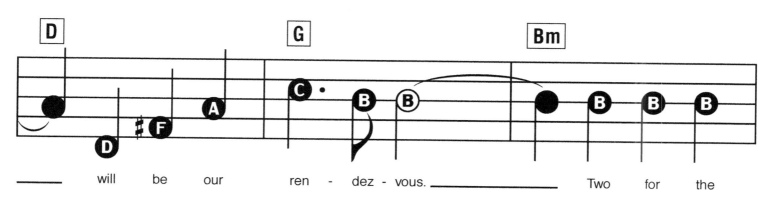

_____ will be our ren - dez - vous. _____ Two for the

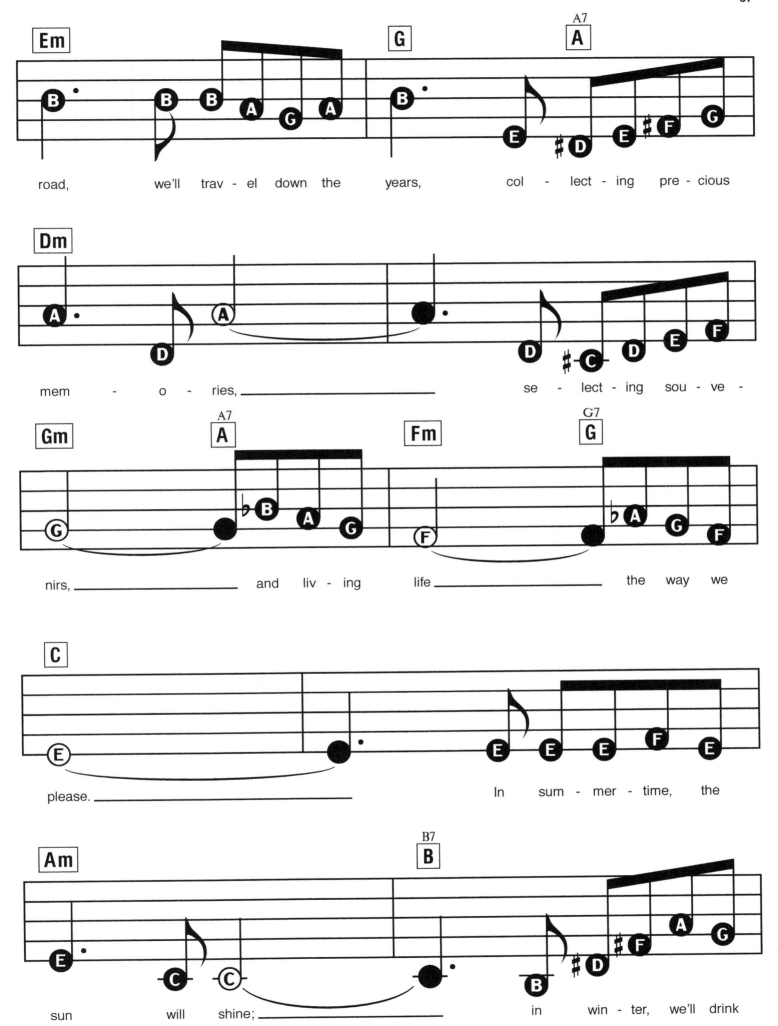

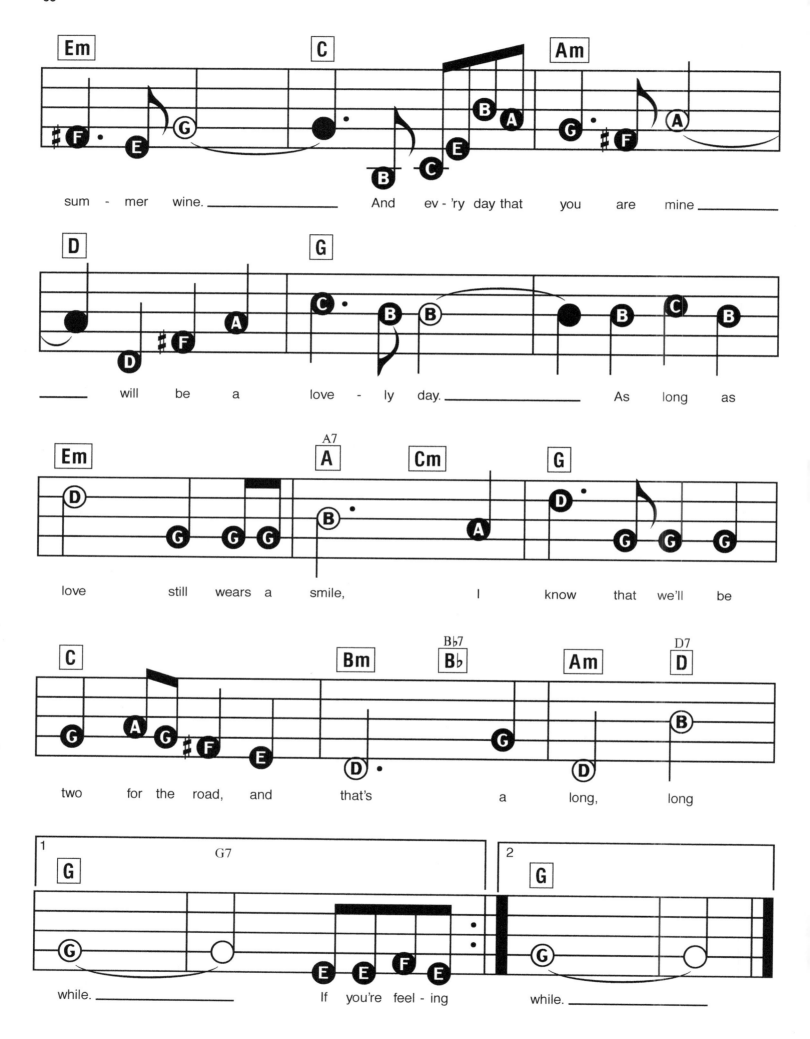

Whistling Away the Dark

Registration 4
Rhythm: Waltz

Words by Johnny Mercer
Music by Henry Mancini

Of - ten I think this sad old
Of - ten I think my poor old

world is whis - tling in the
heart has giv - en up for

dark. _____
good. _____

Just like a child, who,
And like then I see a

late from school, walks brave - ly home through the
brand new face, I glimpse some new neigh - bor -

To Coda ✛

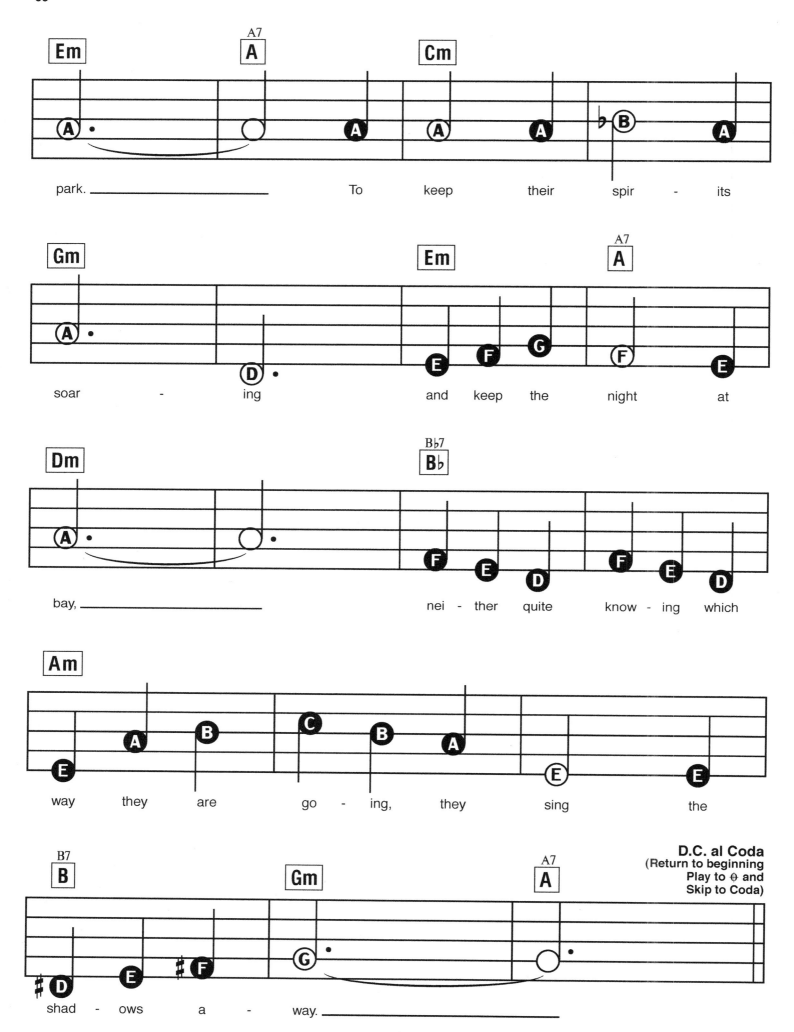

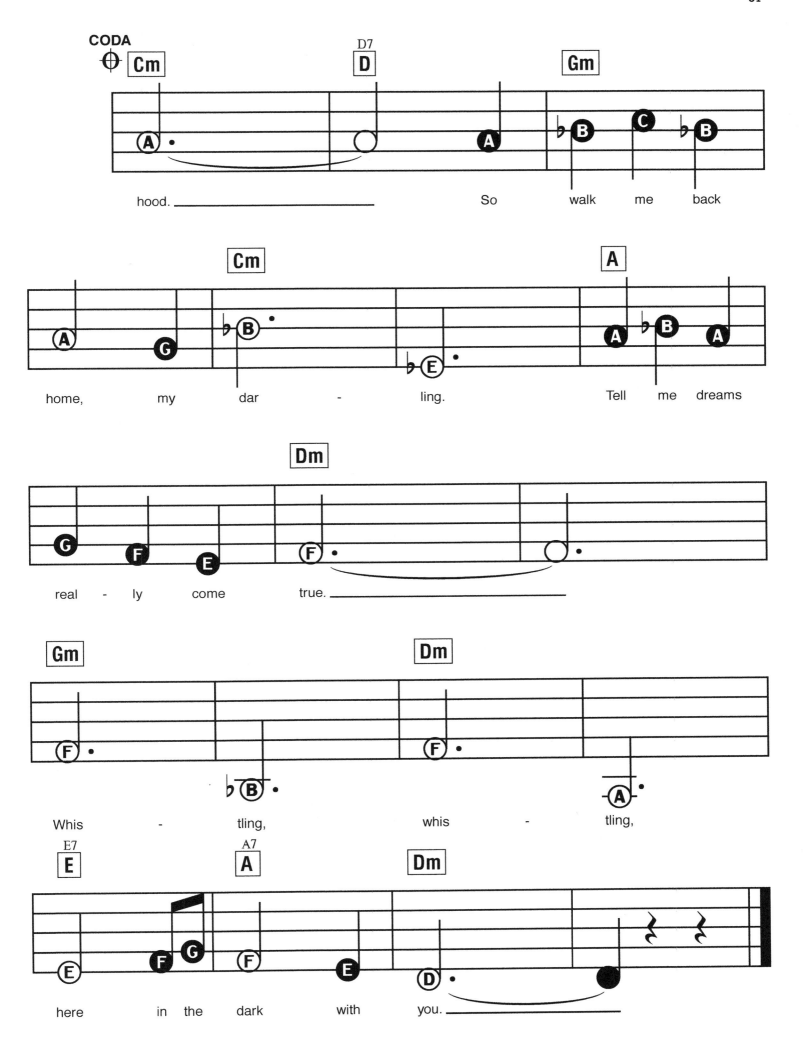

Registration Guide

• Match the Registration number on the song to the corresponding numbered category below. Select and activate an instrumental sound available on your instrument.

• Choose an automatic rhythm appropriate to the mood and style of the song. (Consult your Owner's Guide for proper operation of automatic rhythm features.)

• Adjust the tempo and volume controls to comfortable settings.

Registration

1	Mellow	Flutes, Clarinet, Oboe, Flugel Horn, Trombone, French Horn, Organ Flutes
2	Ensemble	Brass Section, Sax Section, Wind Ensemble, Full Organ, Theater Organ
3	Strings	Violin, Viola, Cello, Fiddle, String Ensemble, Pizzicato, Organ Strings
4	Guitars	Acoustic/Electric Guitars, Banjo, Mandolin, Dulcimer, Ukulele, Hawaiian Guitar
5	Mallets	Vibraphone, Marimba, Xylophone, Steel Drums, Bells, Celesta, Chimes
6	Liturgical	Pipe Organ, Hand Bells, Vocal Ensemble, Choir, Organ Flutes
7	Bright	Saxophones, Trumpet, Mute Trumpet, Synth Leads, Jazz/Gospel Organs
8	Piano	Piano, Electric Piano, Honky Tonk Piano, Harpsichord, Clavi
9	Novelty	Melodic Percussion, Wah Trumpet, Synth, Whistle, Kazoo, Perc. Organ
10	Bellows	Accordion, French Accordion, Mussette, Harmonica, Pump Organ, Bagpipes